Coding & Logic STEM Activity Book for Kids

Table of Contents

Table of Contents 2

Disclaimer 3

Introduction 4

The Search for that Elusive Banana 6

Taxi Please 23

Number Key Challenge 43

Loops 57

Nested Loops 67

Conditional Loops 76

Programming Challenges 80

Answers 89

The Search for that Elusive Banana 90

Taxi Please 104

Number Key Challenge - Answers 114

Loops 117

Nested Loops 122

Conditional Loops 126

Programming Challenges 129

Disclaimer

Copyright © 2023

All Rights Reserved.

No part of this book can be transmitted or reproduced in any form including print, electronic, photocopying, scanning, mechanical or recording without prior written permission from the author.

While the author has taken utmost efforts to ensure the accuracy of the written content, all readers are advised to follow information mentioned herein at their own risk. The author cannot be held responsible for any personal or commercial damage caused by information. All readers are encouraged to seek professional advice when needed.

Introduction

It was a lovely day in Miami. Sam was enjoying the baseball game while working from home. Then he heard a beep, after which he was staring at a blue screen of death. The worst possible time this could happen. Sam was despondent and didn't feel like taking it to the repair shop. Sam yelled loudly in frustration. On hearing this, his 8-year-old son asked what happened. On learning about the blue screen, his son told him not to worry. He took the laptop and started diagnosing the problem. He checked for any hardware issues and verified that there were no issues there. He restarted the computer and did a complete software scan. He uninstalled a malfunctioning software that Sam had installed a day earlier. Within 30 minutes, Sam's computer was as good as new. What Sam's son had just demonstrated was logical thinking and step-by-step troubleshooting. These are essential skills for programming as well. These are the skills that you will learn in this book.

This workbook has activities designed to improve your logic and problem-solving abilities! It's the best way to start coding. It's filled with basic exercises that are designed for kids to improve creativity, problem solving, logic and critical thinking. These are more skills that are essential for programming.

It contains a diverse range of exercises, from beginner level scratch arrow programs to loop prediction exercises. It starts off easy to increase engagement and increases in difficulty as one progresses through the book. It unravels the mysteries of coding one step at a time. It allows one to focus on the logic and problem-solving aspect of programming.

While this workbook has been designed for young kids, it can be used by anyone who's struggling to understand the basics of coding.

This workbook is self-paced, and one can progress at a speed that suits then. One can go through this book independently or with the help of a mentor. It's a great place to experiment and learn from them. You ready to get started?

The Search for that Elusive Banana

Below is a series of challenges that are great for those who have never done any coding before, especially young kids. It might seem simple at first, but it's the first basic step to the process of sequential thinking. Sequential thinking forms the basis of programming, where you need to break a problem down into individual parts and solve them one step at a time.

In the challenges below, use arrows below to guide the monkey to the target banana using the shortest path. A lot of these have two possible paths or solutions. Answers to all problems are at the back of the book.

Arrows That Can be Used:

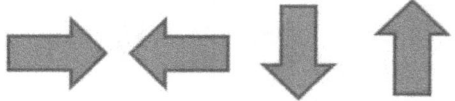

Use the first challenge below and the answer to understand the puzzle.

Challenge 1

Challenge 1 – Answers

Challenge 2

Challenge 3

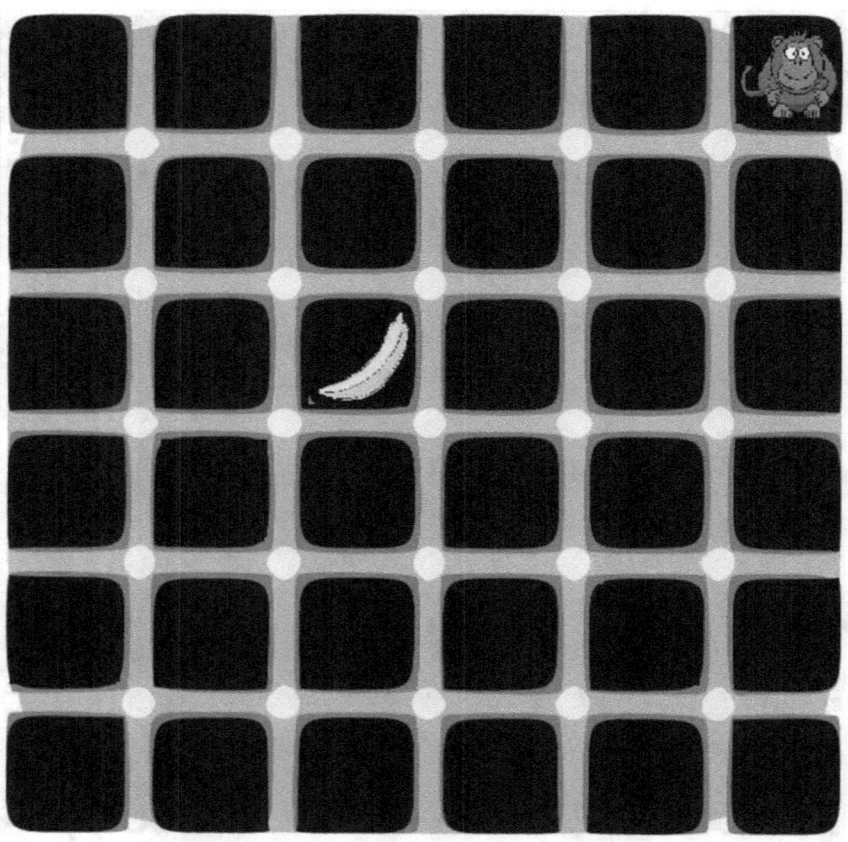

Challenge 4

Challenge 5

Challenge 6

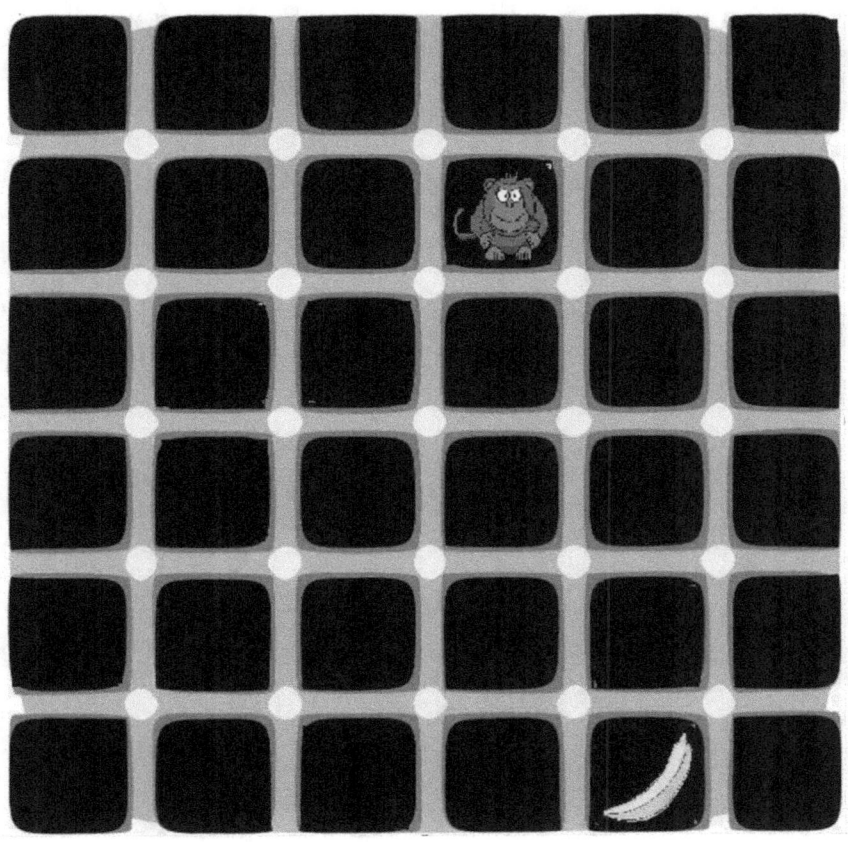

Challenge 7

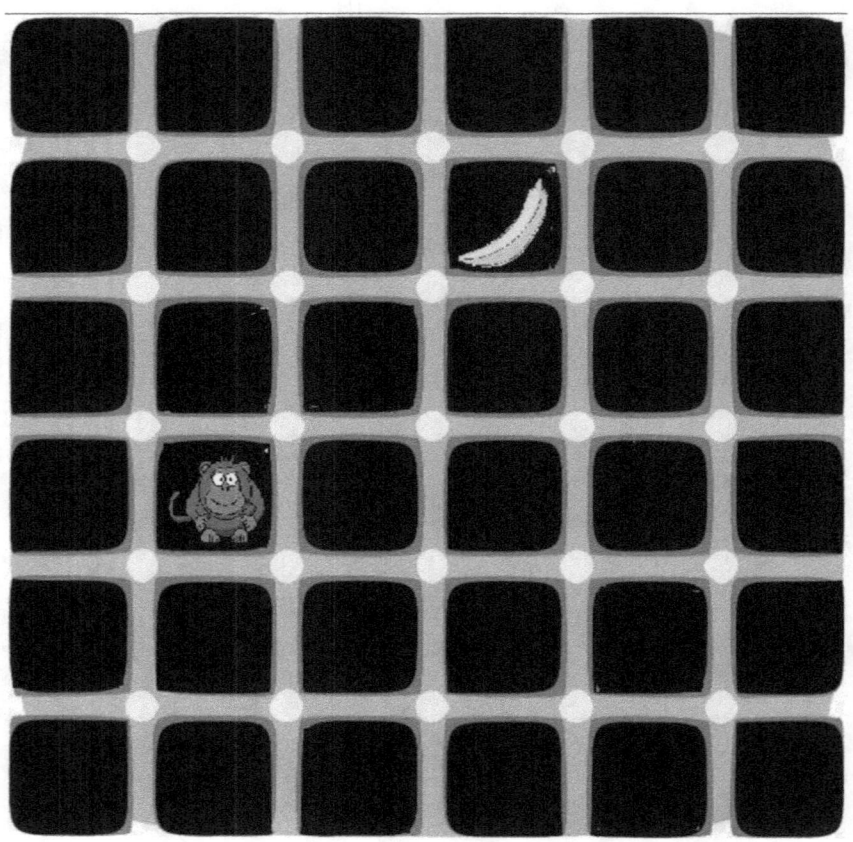

Challenge 8

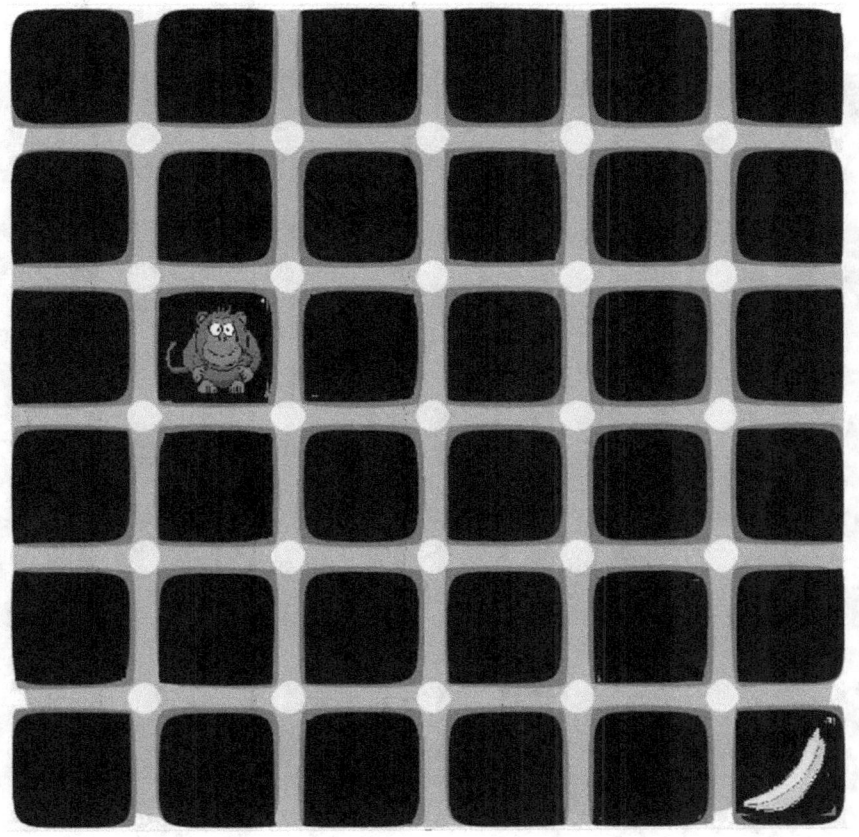

Challenge 9

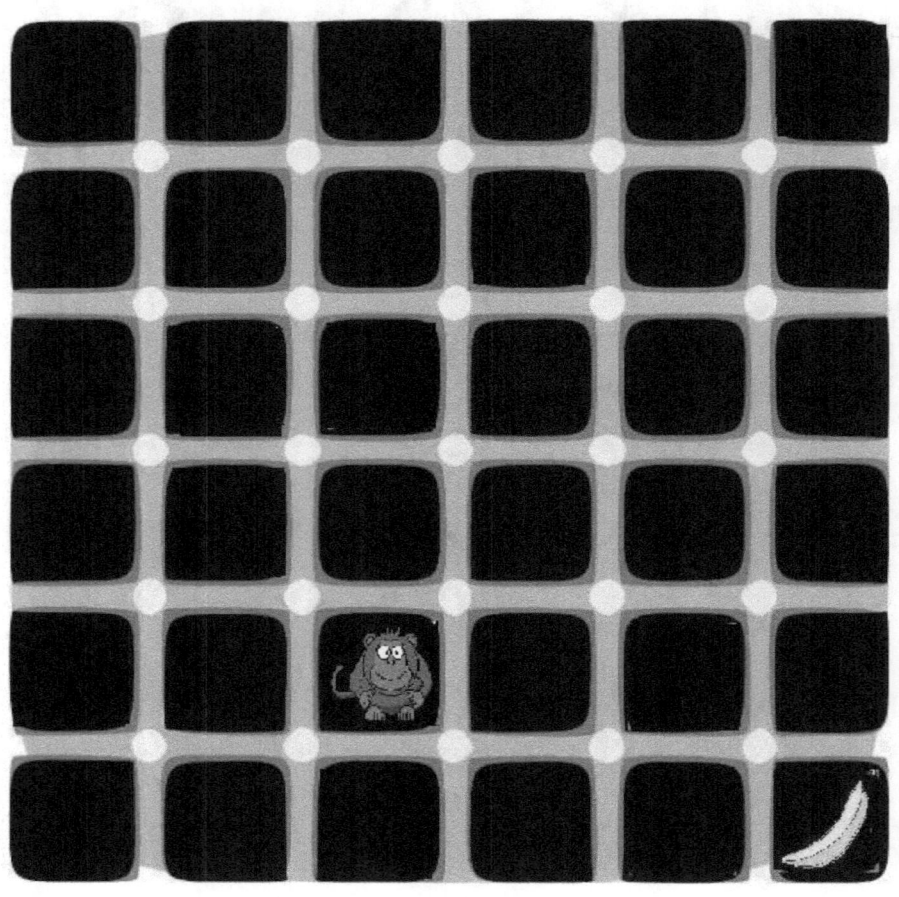

Challenge 10

Now, we have some obstacles in the monkey's path. Find the shortest distance to the banana while avoiding the rocks.

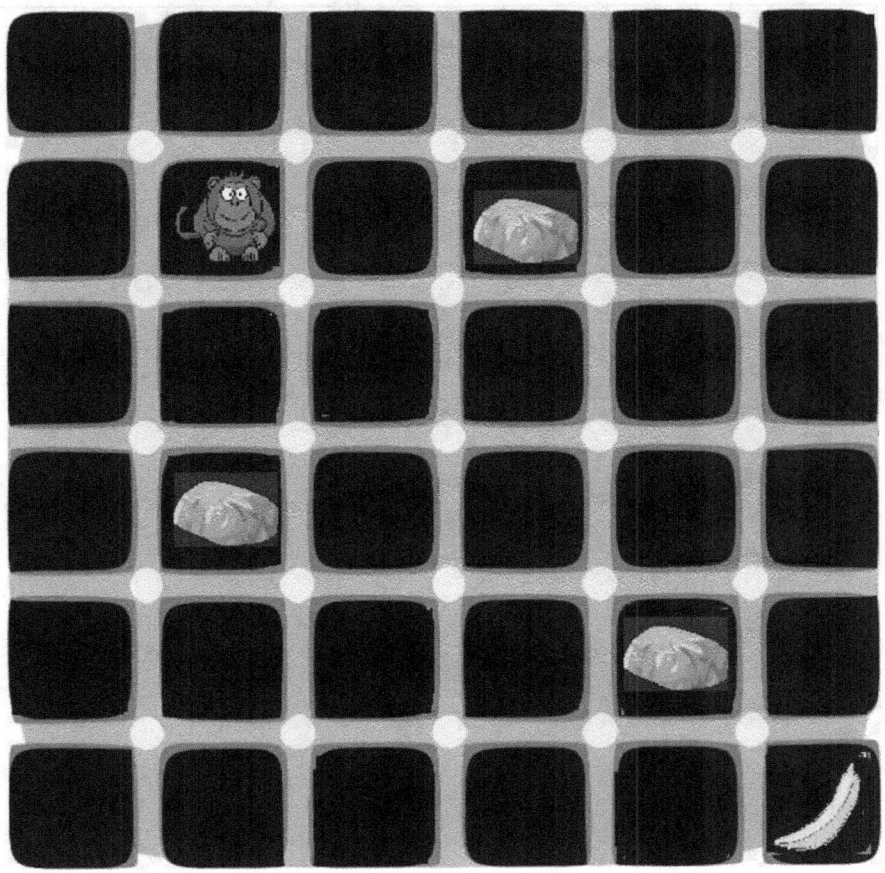

Challenge 11

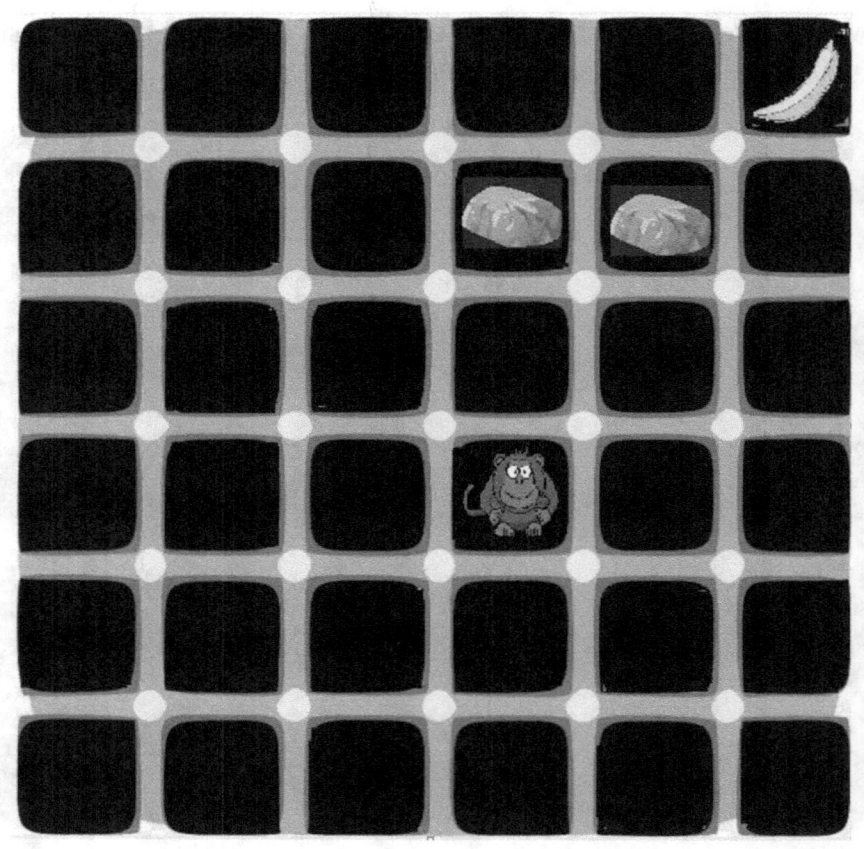

Challenge 12

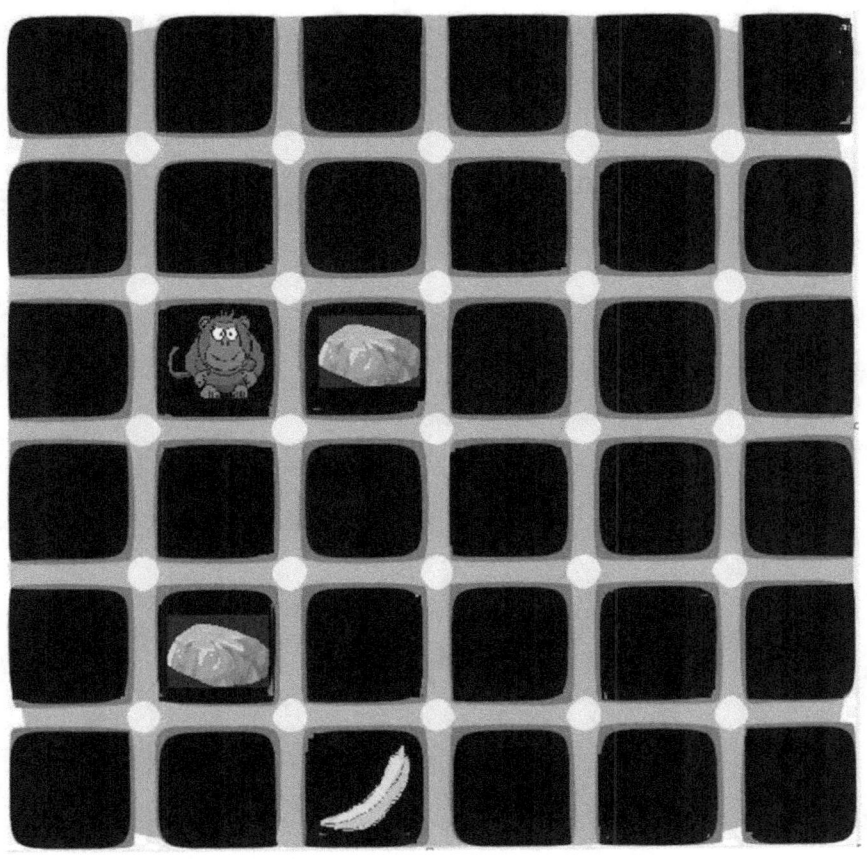

Challenge 13

Challenge 14

Challenge 15

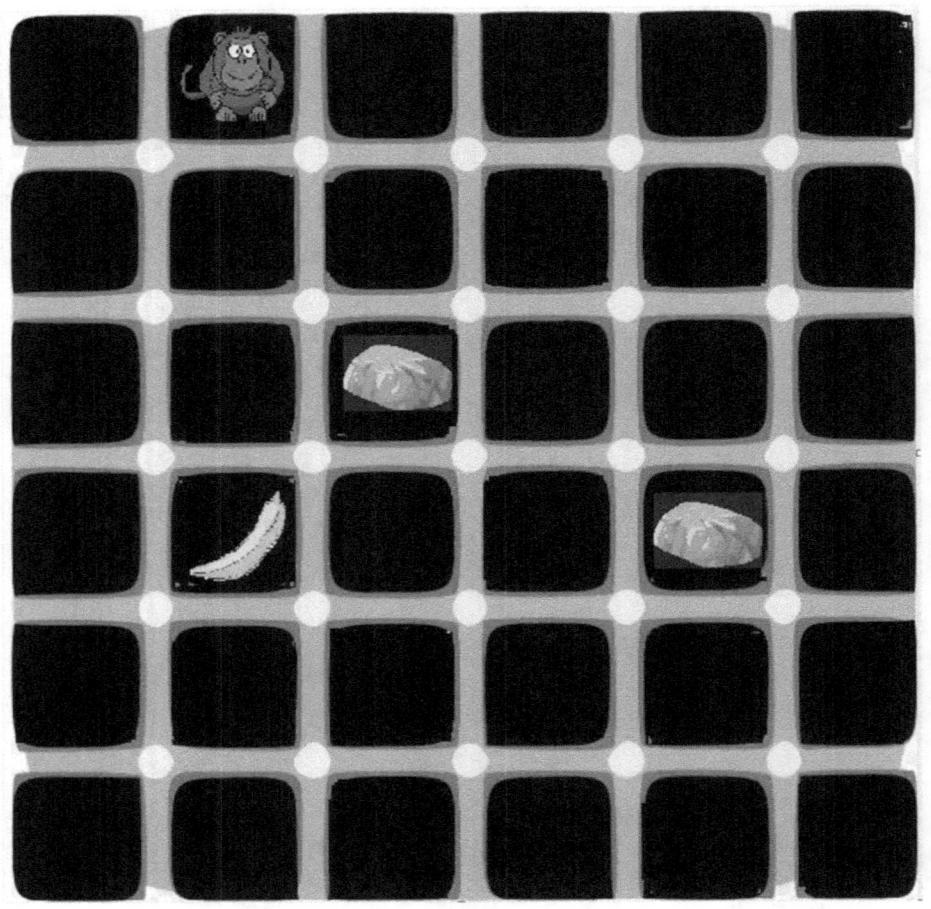

Taxi Please

In the next few challenges, the taxi needs to pick up the woman and give her a ride to her home. Use arrows in the same way as was done for previous challenges to find the shortest path.

Challenge 16

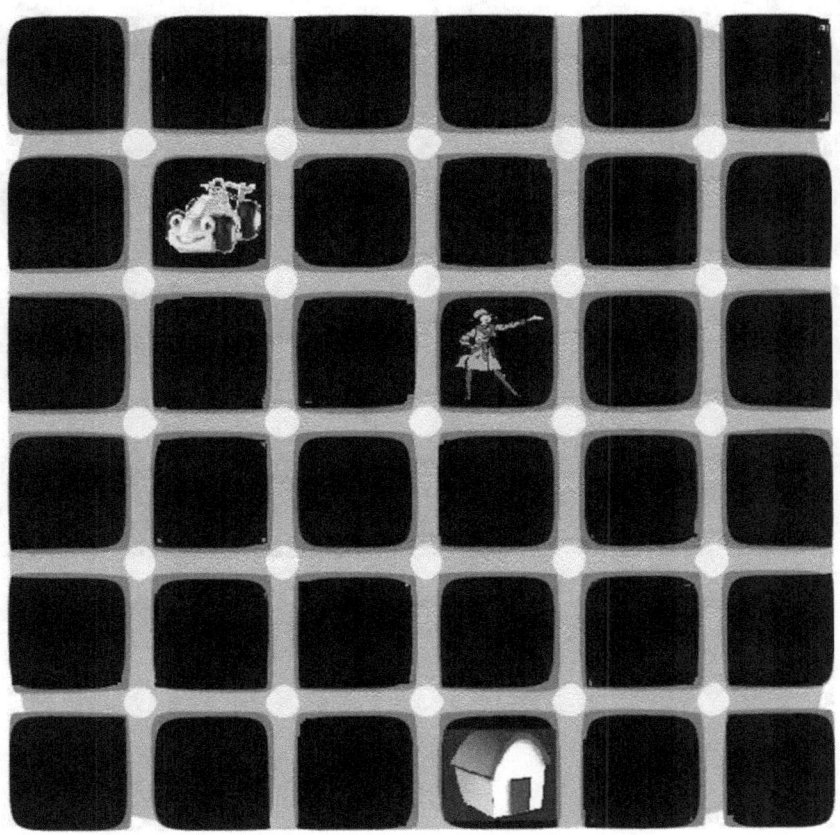

Challenge 17

Challenge 18

Challenge 19

Challenge 20

Challenge 21

Challenge 22

Challenge 23

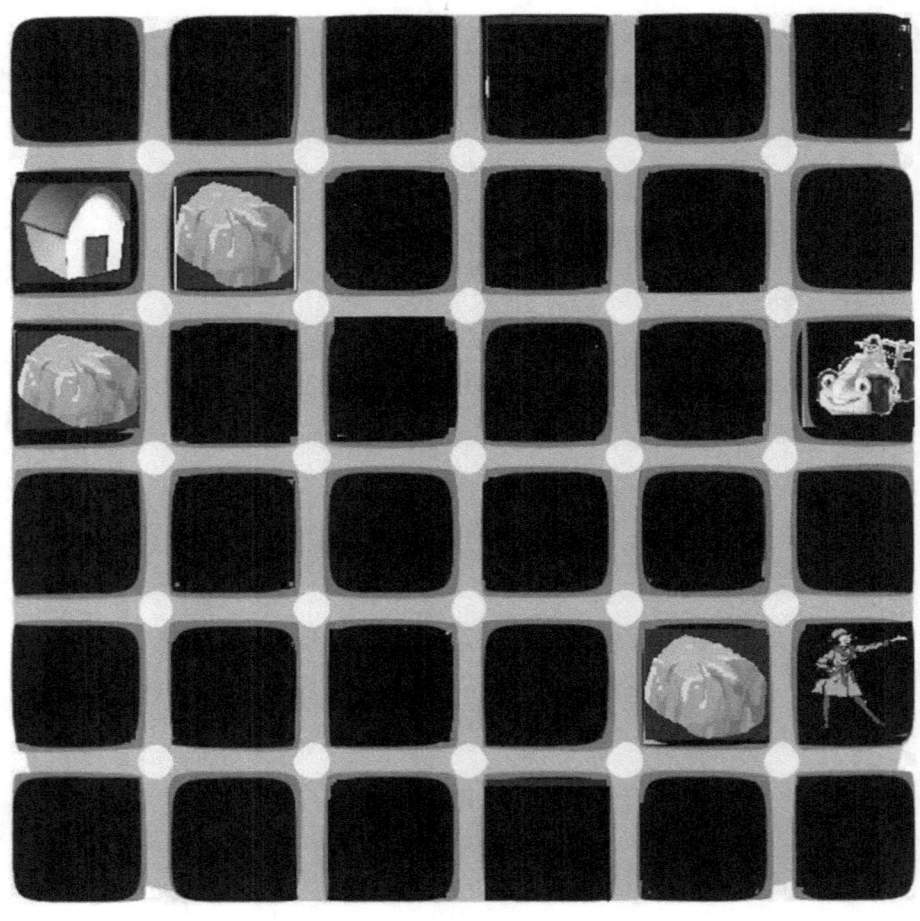

Challenge 24

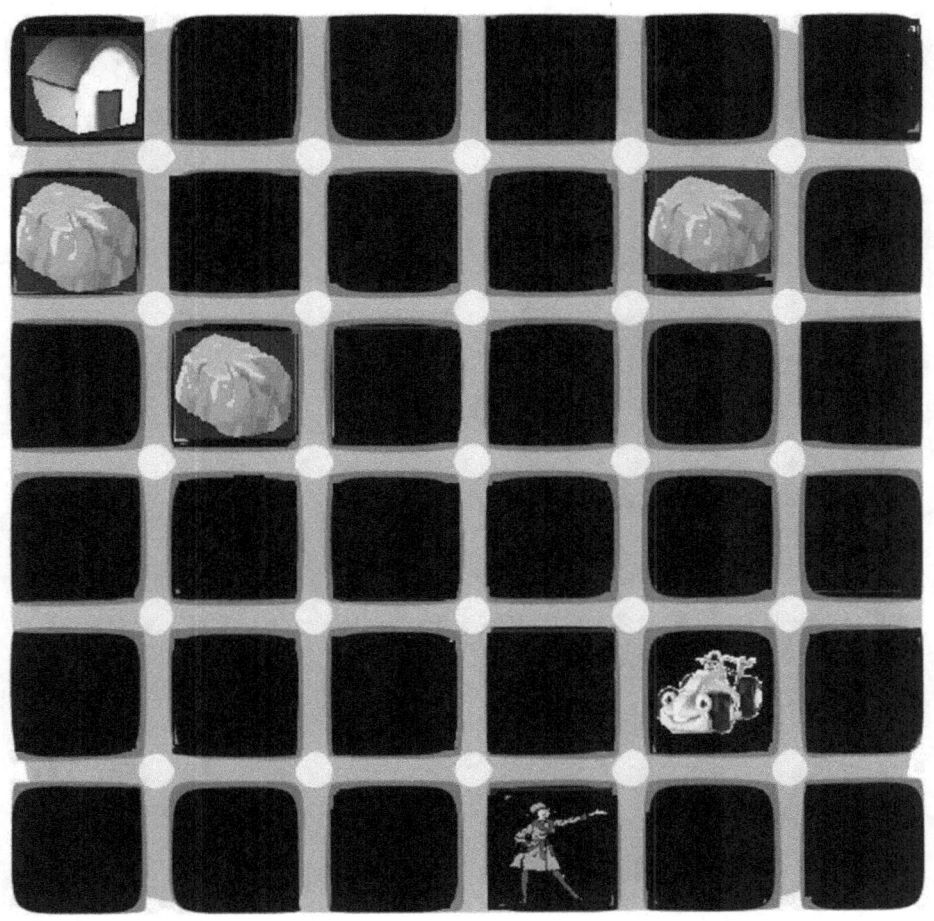

Challenge 25

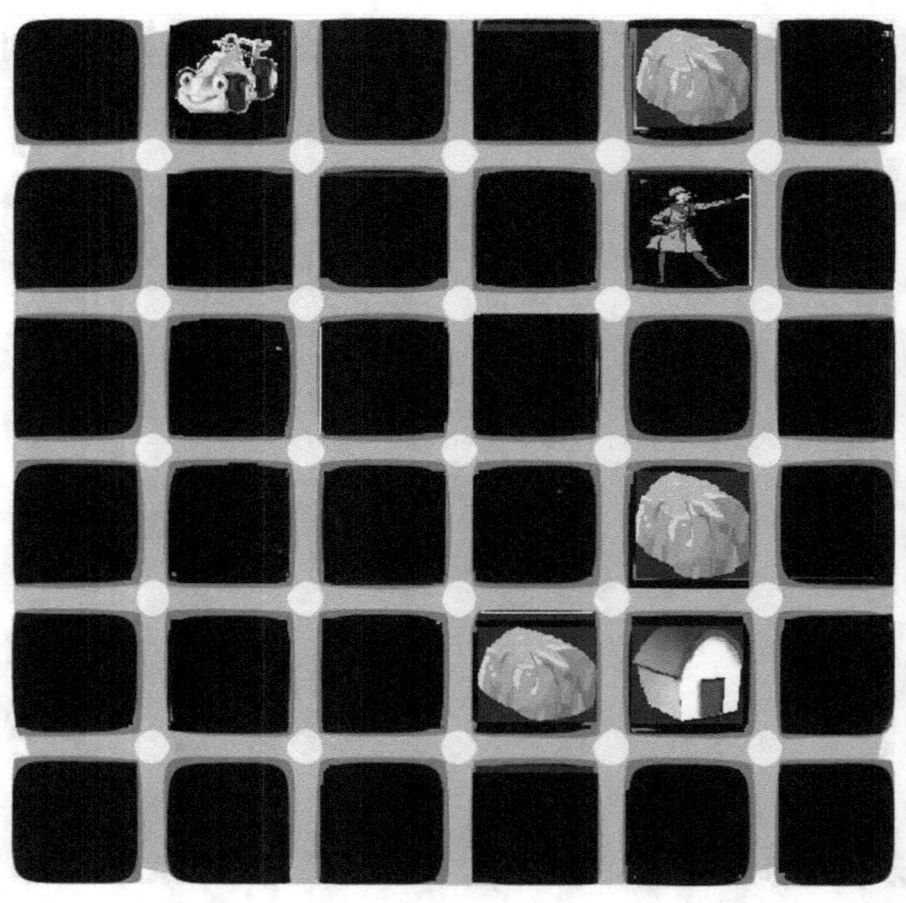

Challenge 26

Challenge 27

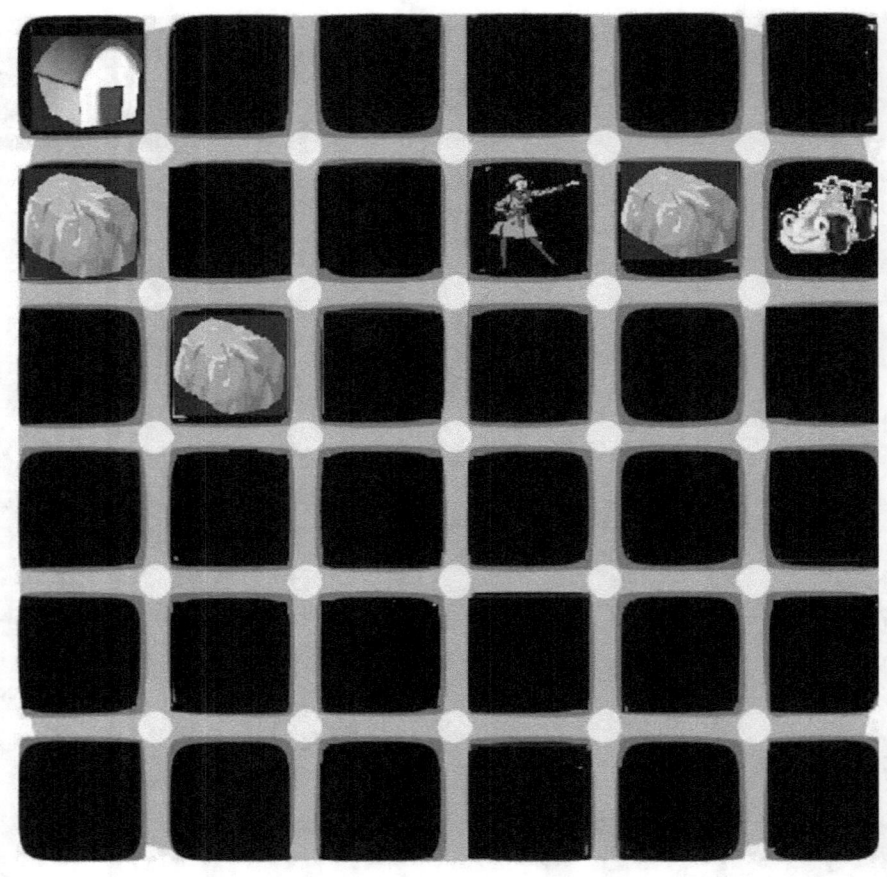

Challenge 28

Challenge 29

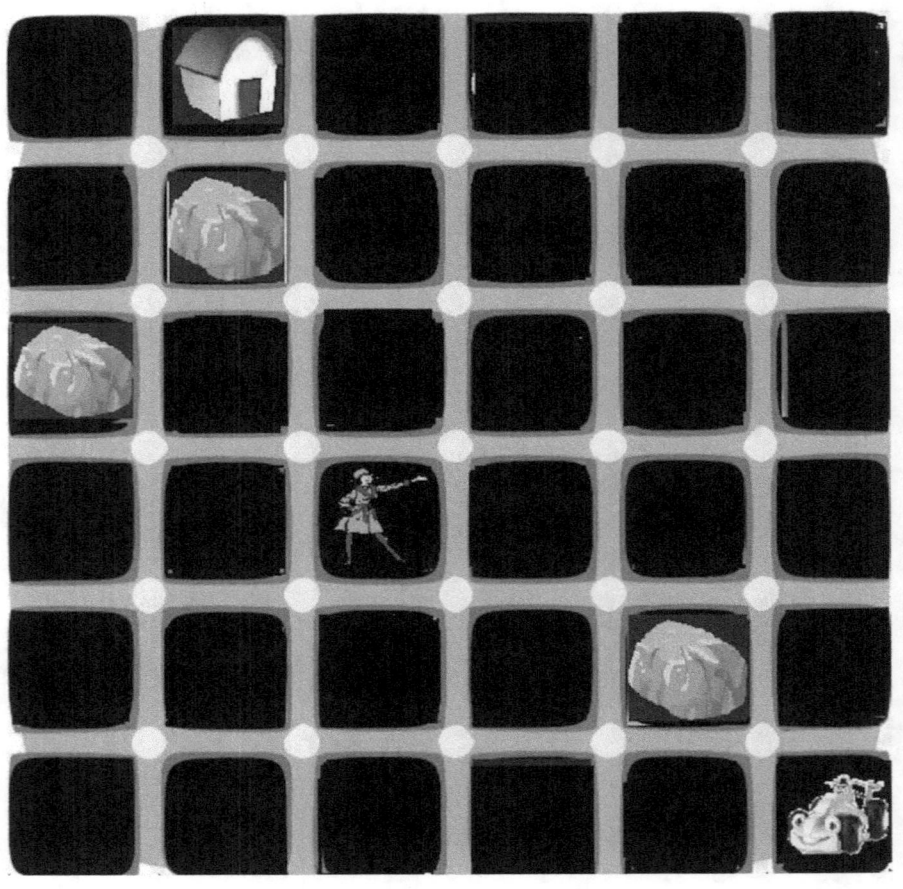

Challenge 30

Challenge 31

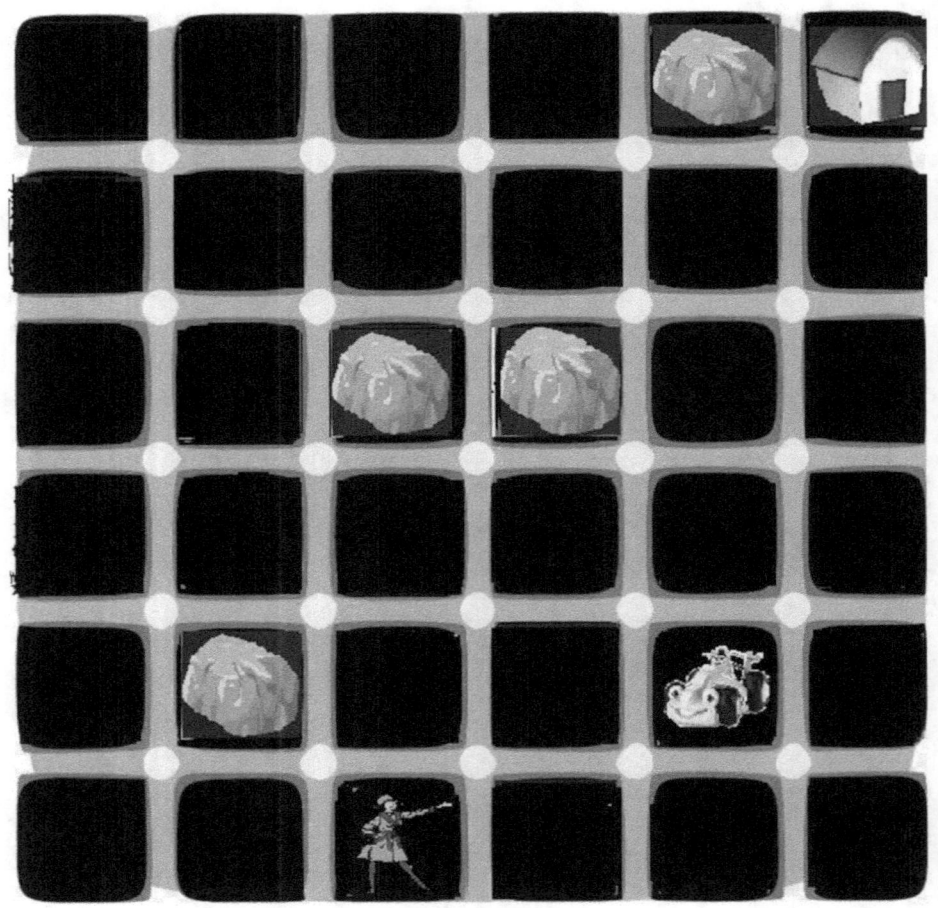

Challenge 32

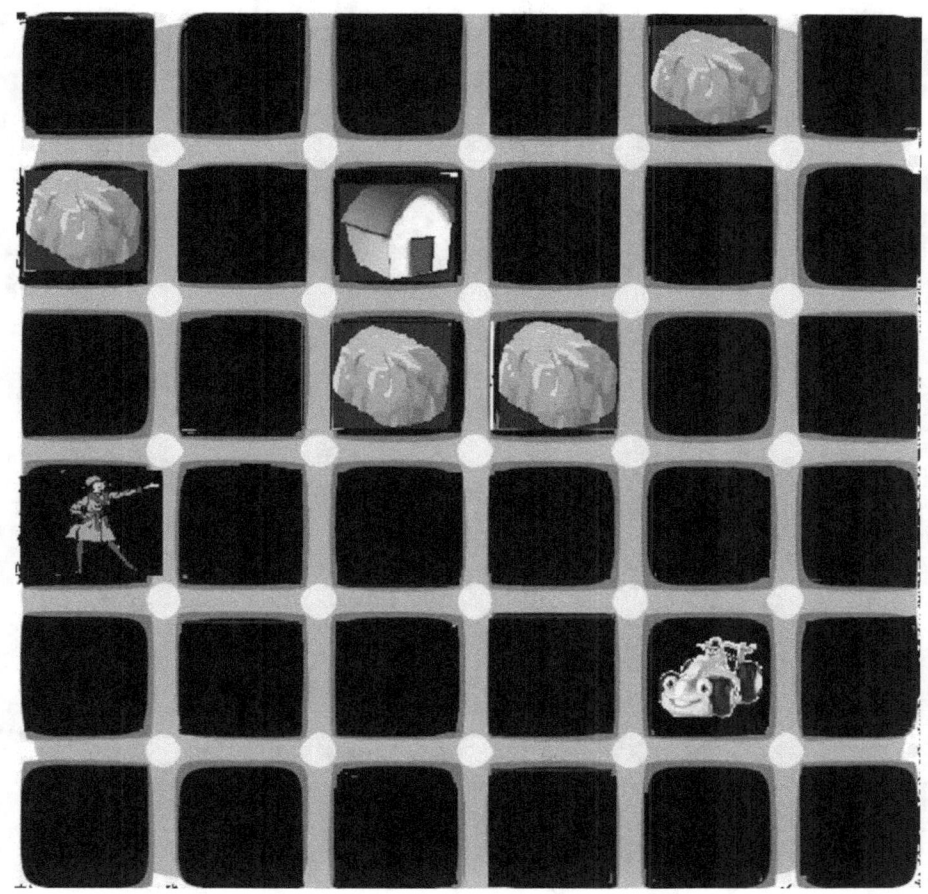

Challenge 33

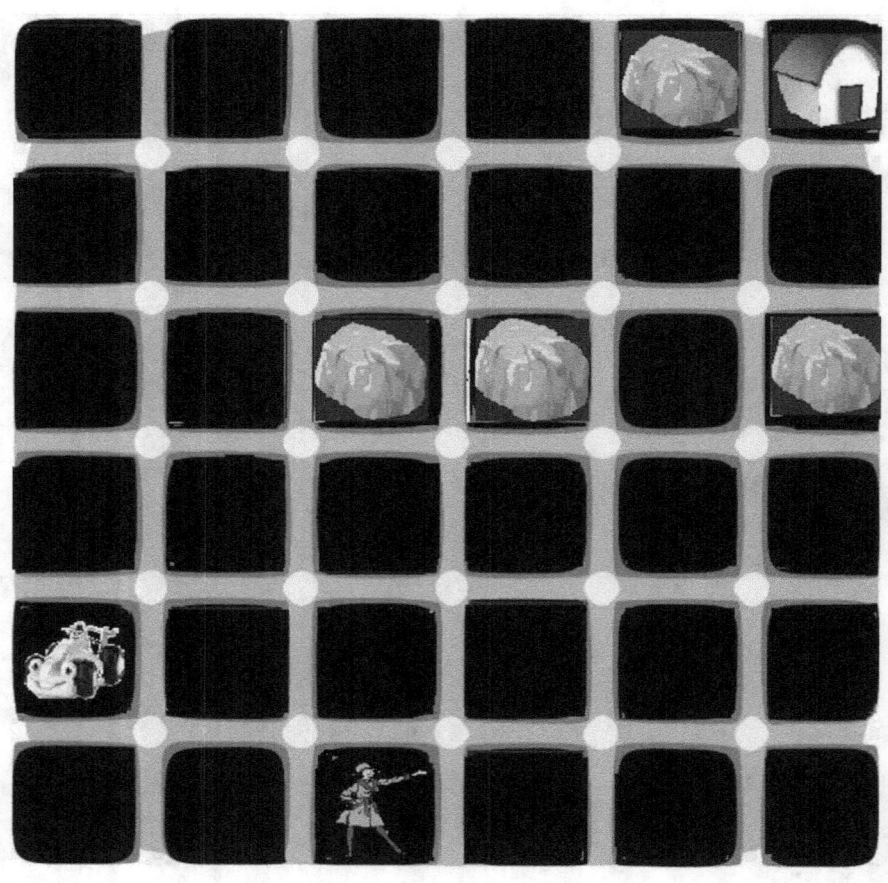

Challenge 34

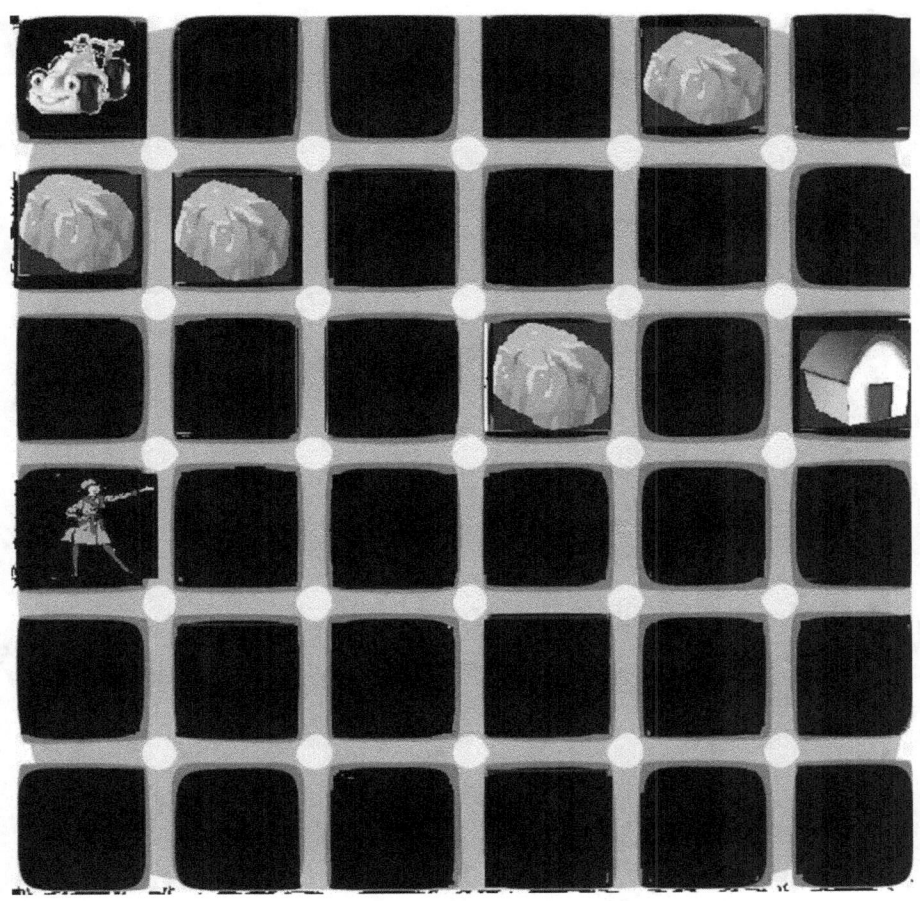

Challenge 35

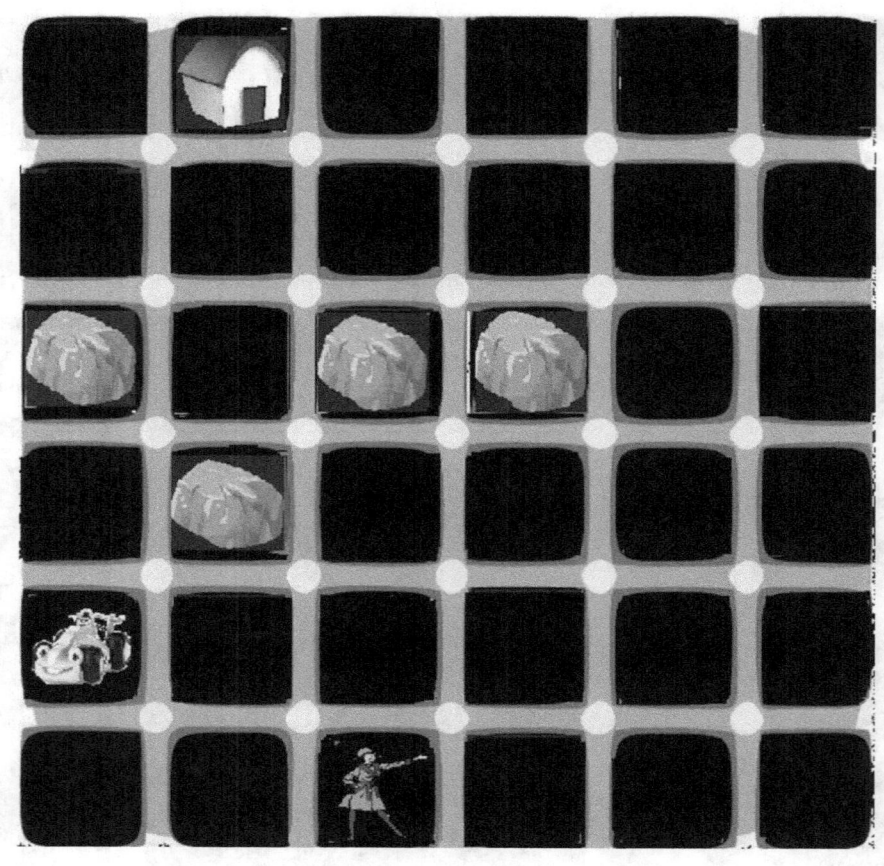

Number Key Challenge

Memorize the keys below and solve the problems that follow. Each digit corresponds to a picture, and this is used as a map for all the problems that follow.

1	ostrich	6	snail
2	palm tree	7	sun
3	monkey	8	elephant
4	flower	9	spider
5	fries	0	zebra

Solve the below simple Math problems using the number key:

Challenge 36-40

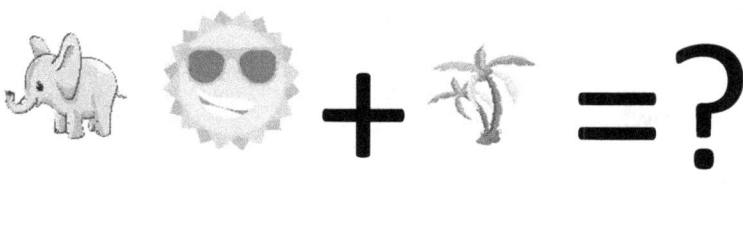

Challenge 41-45

Solve these below:

Challenge 46-55

Find the squares of the following numbers:

Challenge 56-61

Find the remainder below. "%" is the remainder of the first number divided by the second.

For example, 5%2 is the remainder when 5 is divided by 2. So, 5%2 = 1.

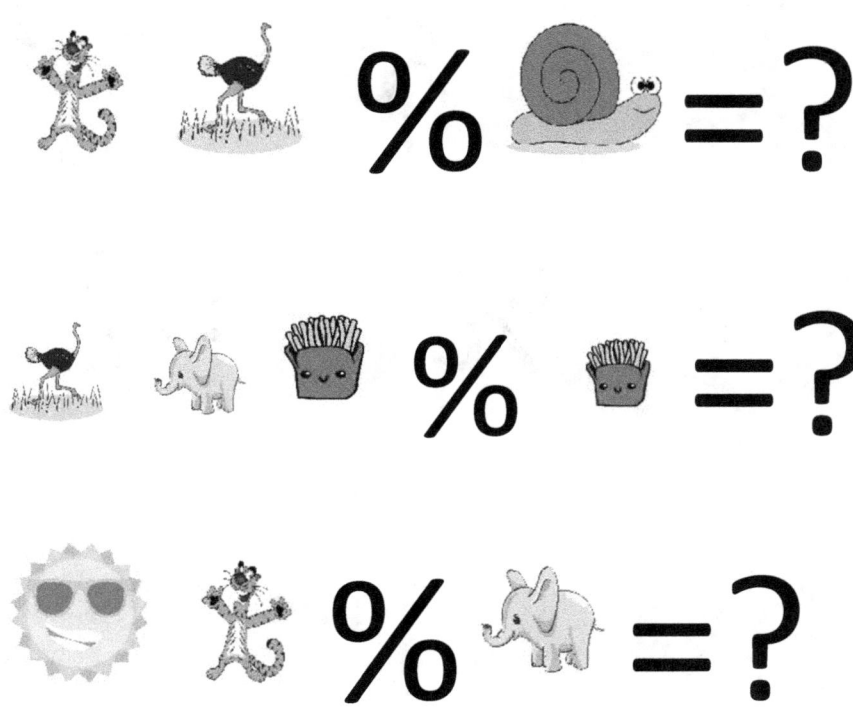

Challenge 62-67

Solve the problems below:

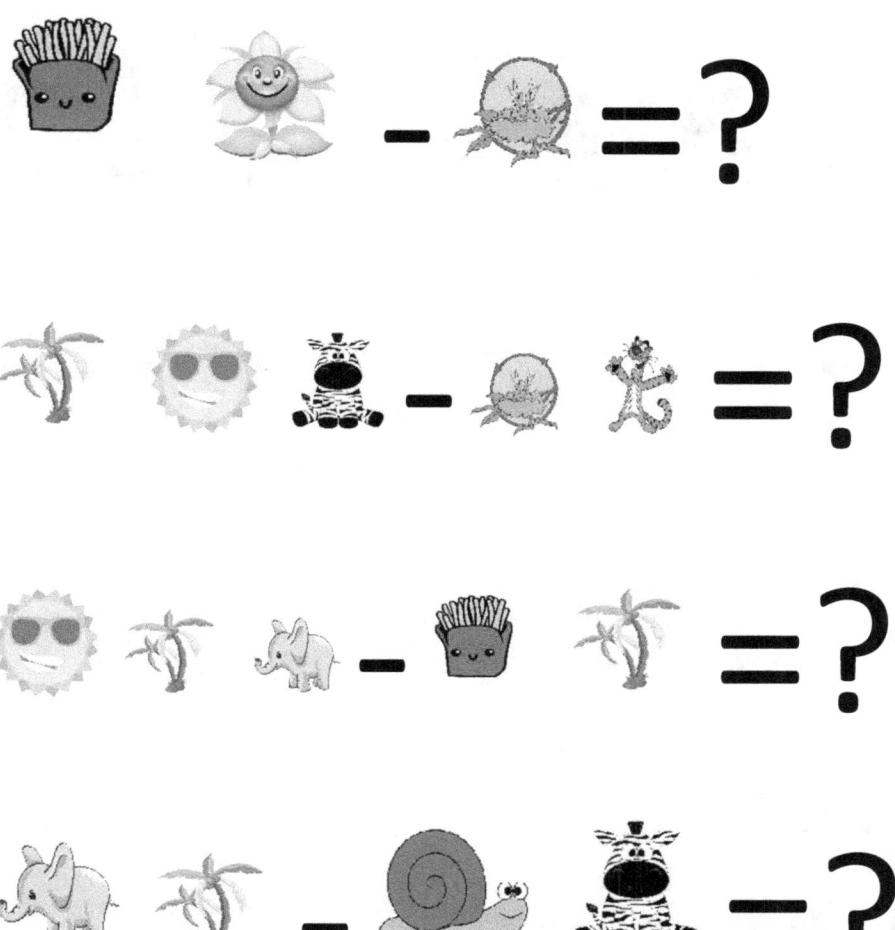

Challenge 68-72

Answer the following multiple-choice questions:

68. Which of the following is not a multiple of 11?

69. Which of the following is a palindrome?

70. Which of the following is a perfect square number?

71. Which of the following is the square root of 16?

72. What year was this book created?

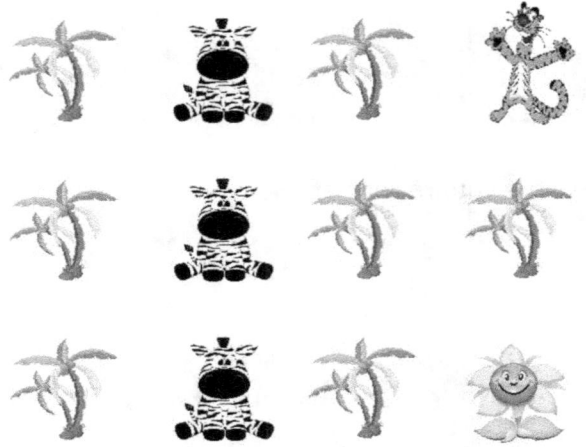

Loops

Imagine you have a toy train, and you want it to go around a toy track multiple times. A loop is just like that track. It assists you in doing something several times without having to repeat the same steps every time.

Let's say you want the train to go around the track five times. Instead of saying, "Okay, train, go around the track one...two...three times...four times...five times," you can use a loop. It's like a special command that tells the train to keep going around the track until it completes five rounds.

So, you can say, "Hey, train, go around the track five times!" The train starts moving and goes around the track once, twice, three times, four times, and finally, five times. The loop helps you avoid saying the same thing repeatedly.

Loops are like magic instructions that make things happen over and over again without getting tired or bored. They are helpful when you have a lot of things to do, and you want the computer or toy to do them automatically.

Let's say you want to print a pattern on the computer screen 1000 times. Without loops, you would have to copy and paste the print instructions again and again till you reach a count of 1000. However, with loops, you can just make a print instruction and put it inside a loop of 1000.

That's what loops are, like a special trick to make things repeat without you having to say or do the same thing again and again.

Example

Now, let's look at a loop with the same example where we print the character "&" 1000 times.

Now, if we didn't use a loop, we would do the following:

print "&"

print "&"

print "&"

print "&"

print "&"

……

Keep going until we do this a 1000 times.

Now, with a loop, we get:

Start of Loop from 1 to 1000:

print "&"

End Loop:

Elements of a Loop

There are 5 main elements of a loop:

A counter

A counter is an item that counts how many times the loop is executed.

Start Point

The start point is the number that the counter starts with.

End Point

The end point is the number that the counter ends with, after which the loop is no longer executed.

Increment

The increment is how much the counter is incremented every time the loop runs.

Loop Contents

The loop contents are the items inside the loop that are executed every time the loop is run.

Now, let's have a look at above elements given the same example again.

Start Loop: ctr = 1 to 1000:

print "&"

ctr = ctr +1;

End Loop:

In the above loop, ctr is the counter. The loop start point is 1 and end point is 1000. The increment is 1.

Here is how the loop works in pictorial form:

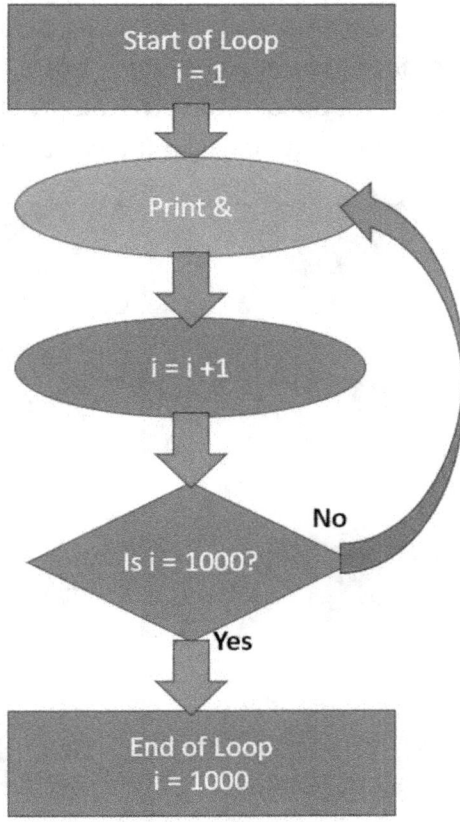

Now, let's have a look at a few simple examples of loops that we can use.

Challenge 73

Complete a loop that prints out all numbers from 1 to 20. The flowchart below that is supposed to solve the problem has missing blanks. Complete the missing blanks in the visual below:

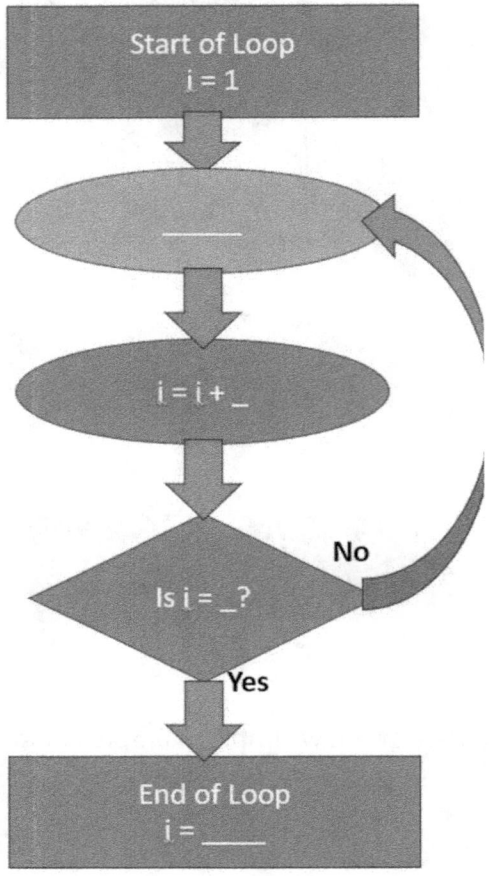

Challenge 74

Complete a loop that prints out all the odd numbers from 1 to 30. Complete the missing blanks in the visual below that aims to solve the problem.

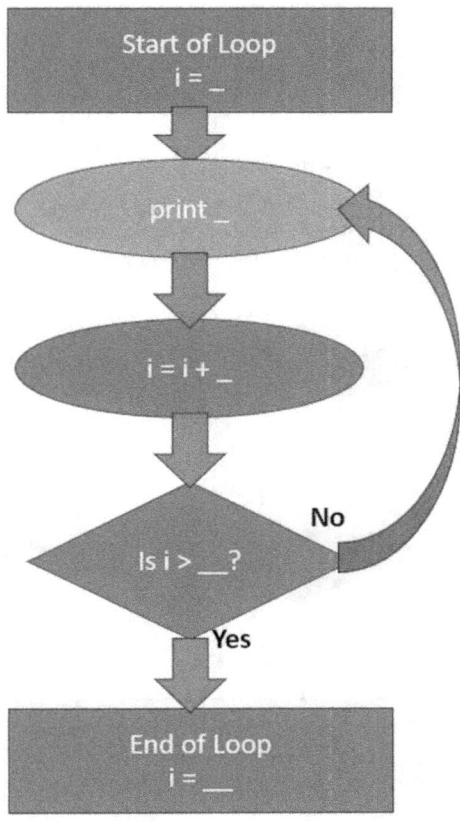

Challenge 75

We need a car to loop around a track 10 times. Part of the car loop is shown in the visual below. Complete the missing blanks in the visual below:

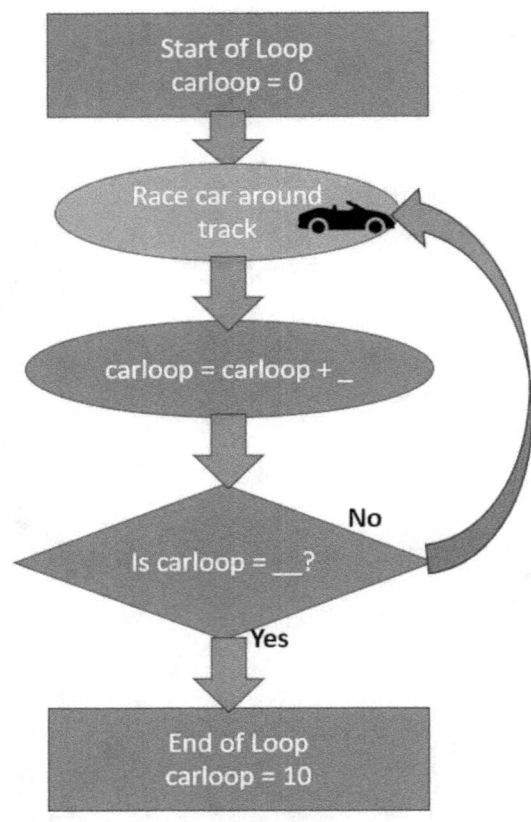

Challenge 76

You oversee a Mars space program. You have a spacecraft that needs to orbit around Mars, but it needs to only do so 5 times. Part of the orbit program is shown in the visual below. Complete the missing blanks in the visual below:

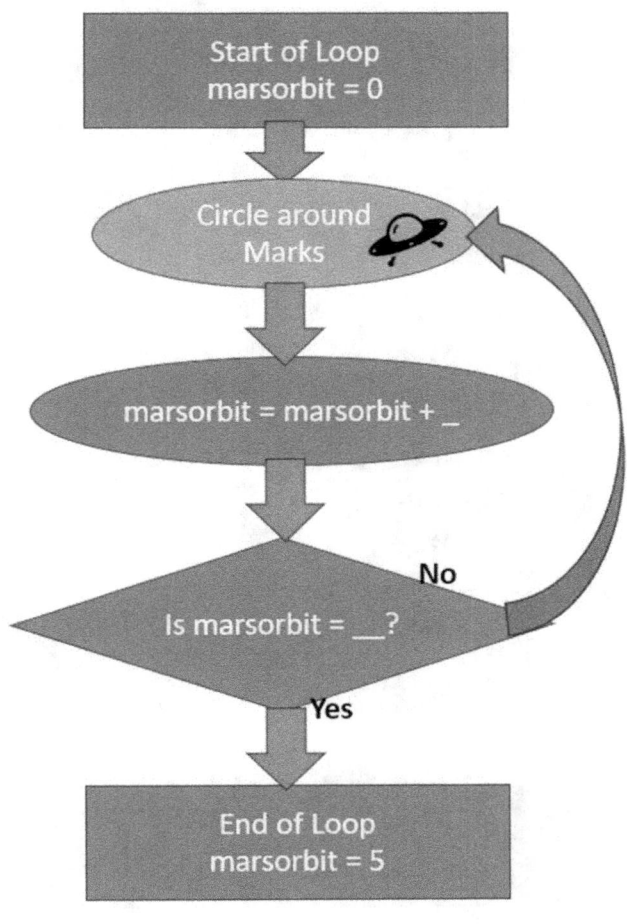

Challenge 77

You are tasked with printing a pattern on the screen 100 times. The pattern has the three characters "(*)". It needs to be printed on a separate line each time. Part of the program is filled out below. Fill out the rest to complete it.

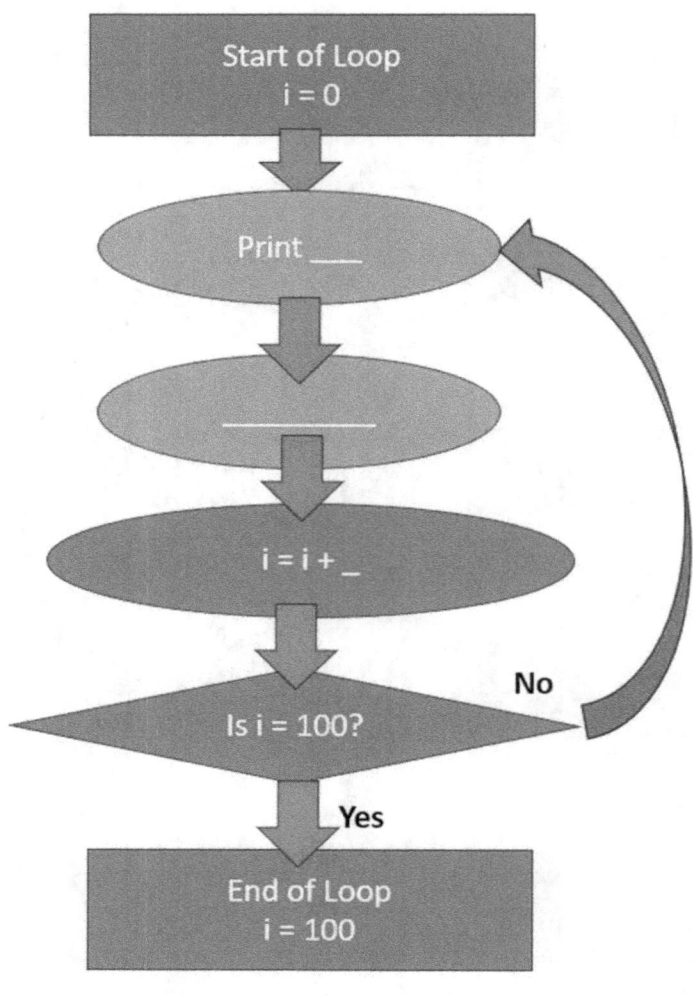

Nested Loops

Now, let's have a look at nested loops. Nested loops are basically loops within a loop. To explain this, let's say you have a box of toy spacecraft. There's supposed to be 10 spacecrafts. Each spacecraft is made of 5 parts. So, you check each toy spacecraft for its 5 parts, then move on to the next one. You do this 10 times till you run out of spacecrafts.

So, what you just completed is a nested loop. The outer loop is the counting of the spacecraft 10 times. Within each loop of counting spacecraft, there is a loop where you check the 5 parts of each spacecraft. This is the inner loop.

The nested loop example is shown below. The green loop is the inner loop where we check the 5 parts of the spacecraft. The blue loop is the outer loop where we count the number of spacecrafts.

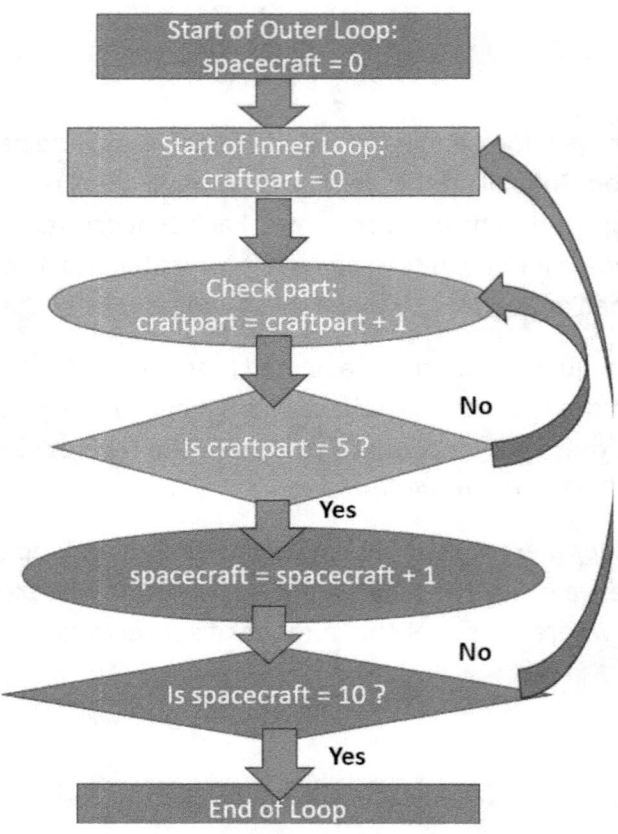

Challenge 78

A car needs to go around a racetrack 100 times. The way you can tell if it completes a lap is when the car completes 3 bends, as each lap has 3 bends in it. Use a nested loop to keep track of the number of times the car goes around the track, till it reaches 100 laps.

The below diagram helps achieve this objective, but it is missing a few blanks. Fill in the blanks to complete this task.

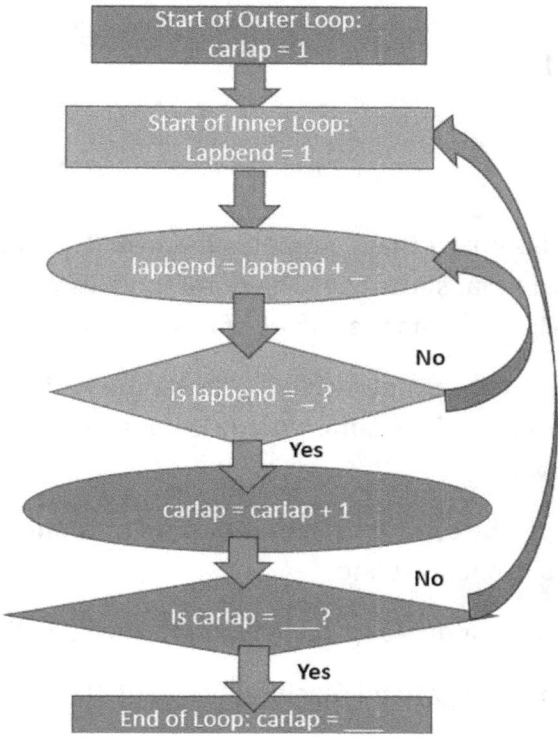

Challenge 79

Print the sum of numbers from 1 to a certain number. For example, if the number is two, print the number 3 (1+2). Do this for the first 10 numbers and move onto the next line each time. The output is below:

1

3 (1+2)

6 (1+2+3)

10 (1+2+3+4)

....

...

Below is the flowchart that completes the task. The outer loop has a counter called i that starts at 1. The outer loop also has a sum counter called sum which counts the values of the inner loop.

The inner loop has a counter called j. Each time j is increased, it is added to the value of the sum. When j is equal to the value of i, the inner loop ends.

i is incremented by 1, and the sum is printed onto the screen and the cursor moves to the next line.

Then we start the inner loop again with j=1 and sum=0.

The outer loop ends when i reaches a value of 10.

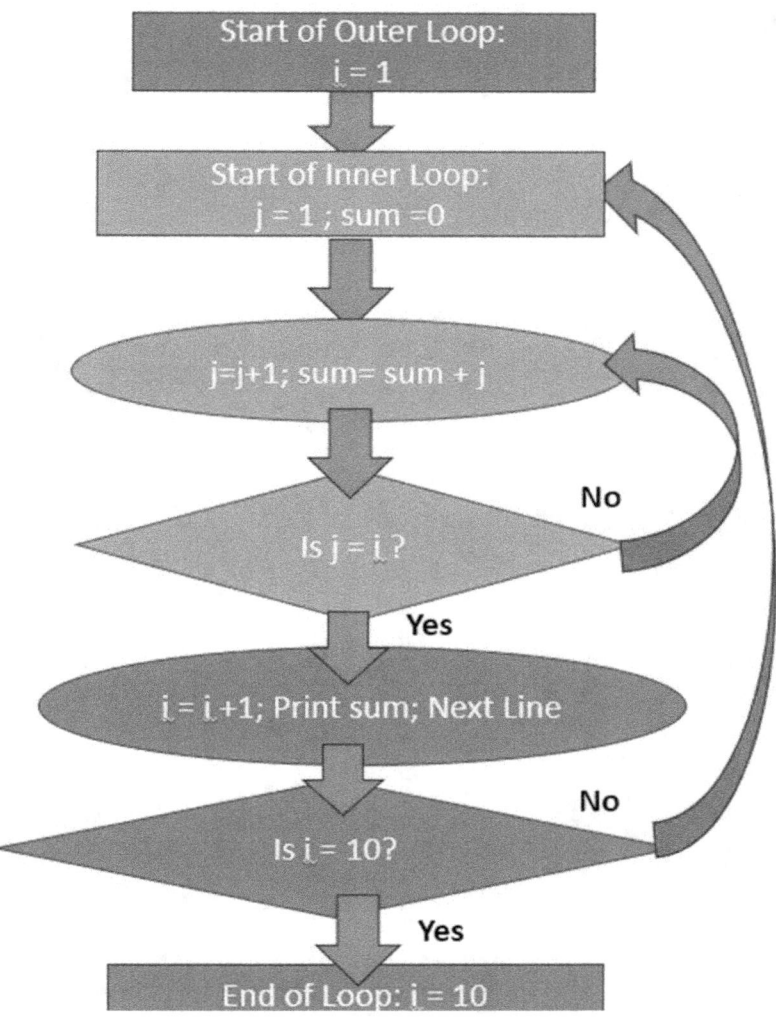

The challenge for this problem is to complete the output of the program above. We'll fill out the first three numbers, but you need to fill out the 7 numbers that follow:

Output:

1

3

6

—

—

—

—

—

—

—

Challenge 80

Print the numbers from 1 to 10 in a sequential fashion. For example, the first line is 1. The second line is 1 2. The third line is 1 2 3. This is best achieved using nested loops. The output is below:

1

1 2

1 2 3

1 2 3 4

1 2 3 4 5

1 2 3 4 5 6

1 2 3 4 5 6 7

1 2 3 4 5 6 7 8

1 2 3 4 5 6 7 8 9

1 2 3 4 5 6 7 8 9 10

Below is the flowchart that will make it happen. Fill in the missing blanks to complete this task:

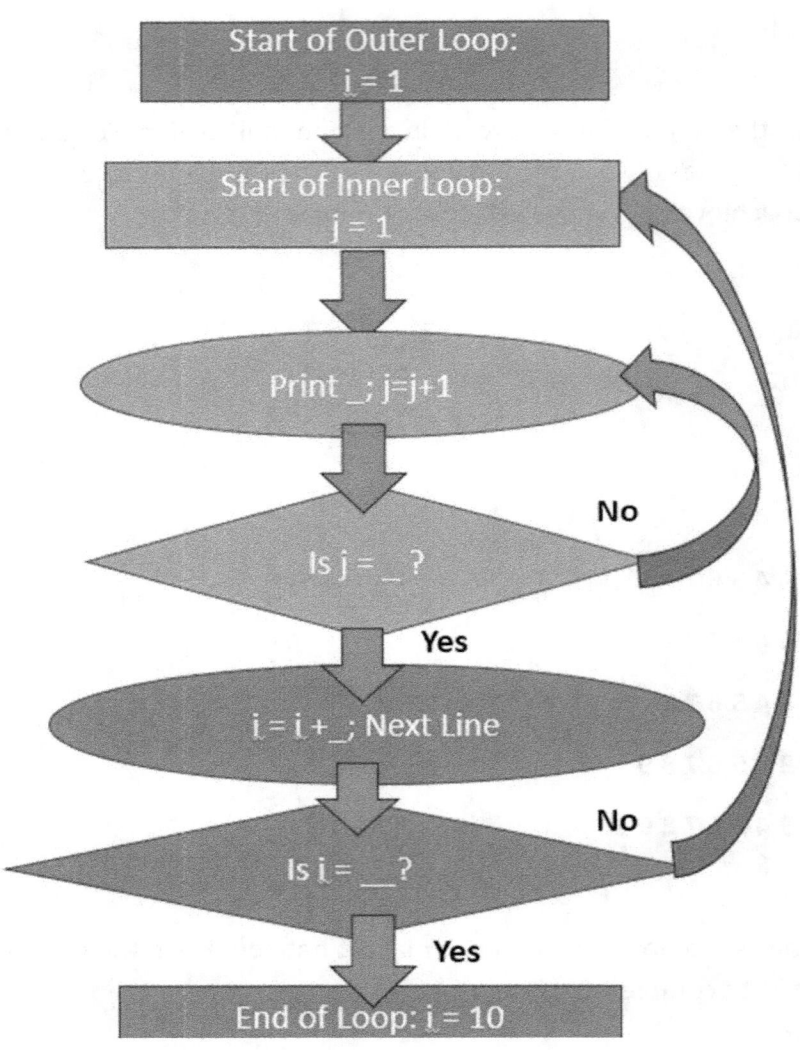

Challenge 81

Print this output on the screen below:

*

* *

* * *

* * * *

* * * * *

So, there's 5 lines of this pattern. Complete the chart below that will achieve this goal.

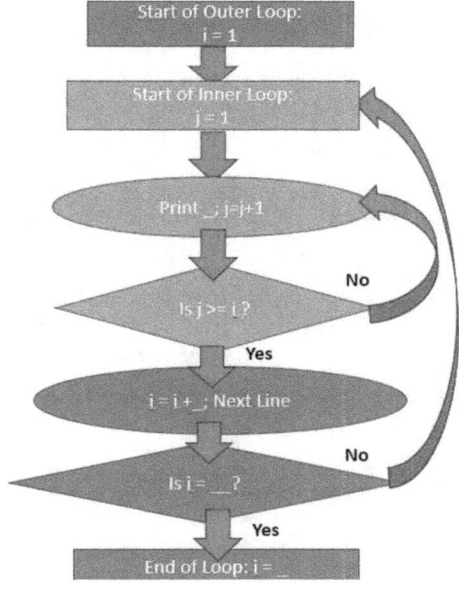

Conditional Loops

A conditional loop is a loop that is executed until a certain condition is met. For example, let's say that you want to orbit a spacecraft around Mars till it runs out of fuel. The loop orbits the spacecraft with a condition inside it. The condition is the check for fuel, and the spacecraft stops orbiting as soon as the fuel is below a certain level.

Here's an example of how the spacefuel conditional loop works.

The loop starts with a spacefuel value of 1000. The loop orbits mars and checks spacefuel. At the end of each orbit, spacefuel is checked to see if it is below 10. If it is below 10, the spacecraft leaves orbit to refuel.

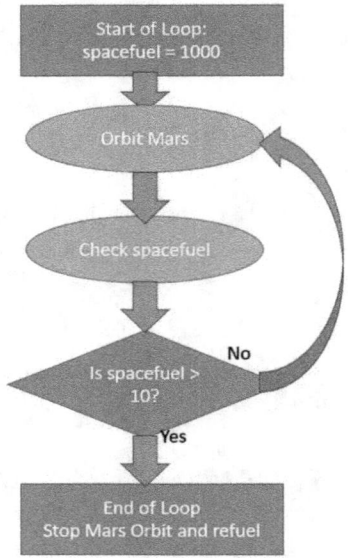

Challenge 82

Write a conditional loop for the toss of a coin. The loop keeps going until the number of heads is 5.

Below is a flowchart of the loop which is incomplete. Fill in the blanks to complete this.

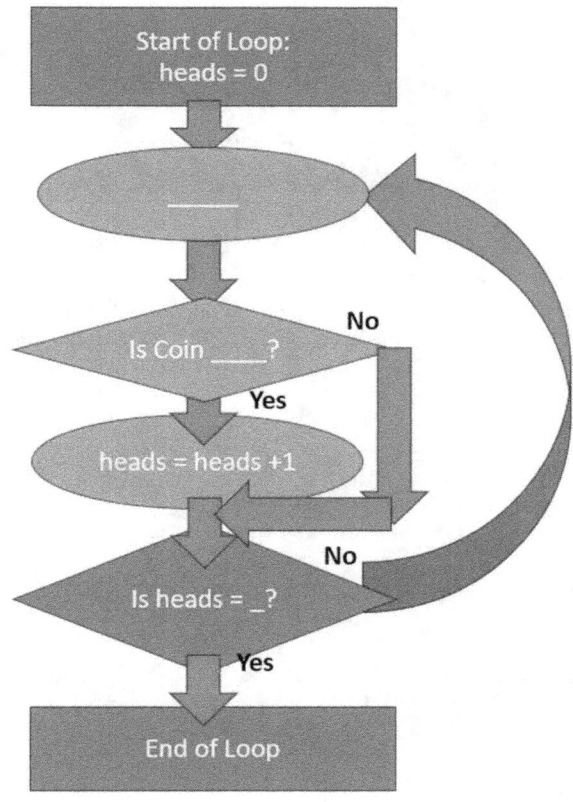

Challenge 83

Create a loop that checks a car's tires after each loop of a racetrack and stops when the car thread is below 2 mm due to wear, to go to a pitstop and change tires.

Below is the loop that is incomplete. Fill in the blanks to complete the loop.

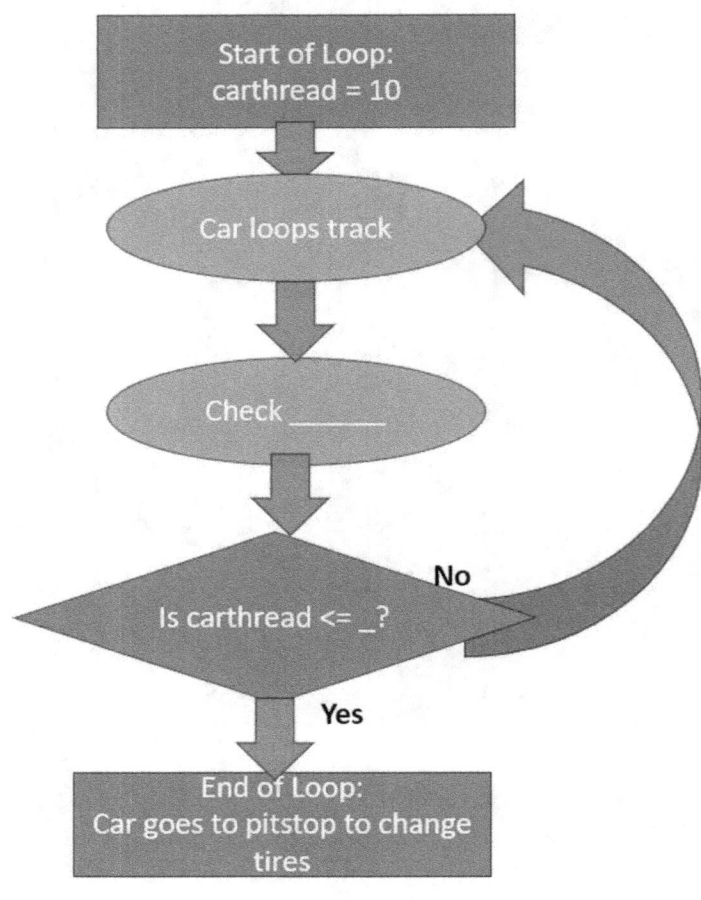

Challenge 84

You are working for a credit card company. You are tasked with designing a loop for each customer that alerts the customer when his credit balance is below $100. Design a loop that checks if a customer's account credit card balance is below $100 after each transaction. The loop stops when this happens.

The incomplete conditional loop is below. Fill in the blanks to complete.

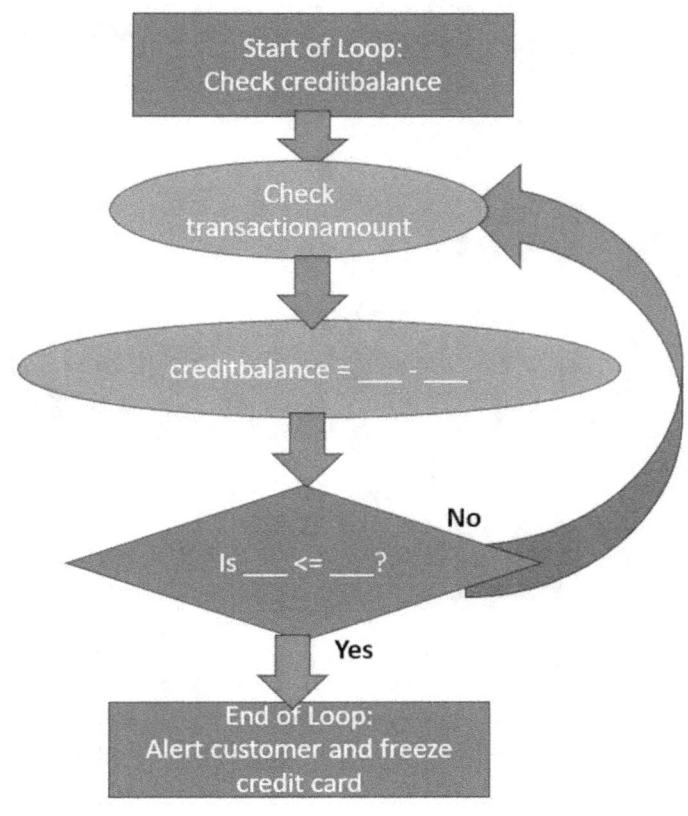

Programming Challenges

Find the outputs for the following loops:

Challenge 85

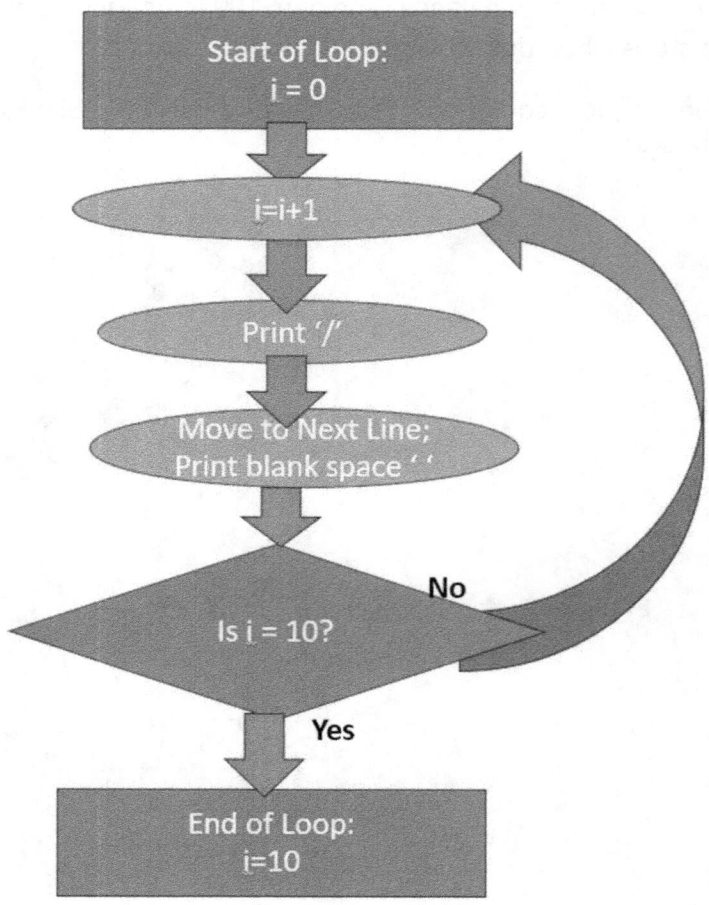

Challenge 86

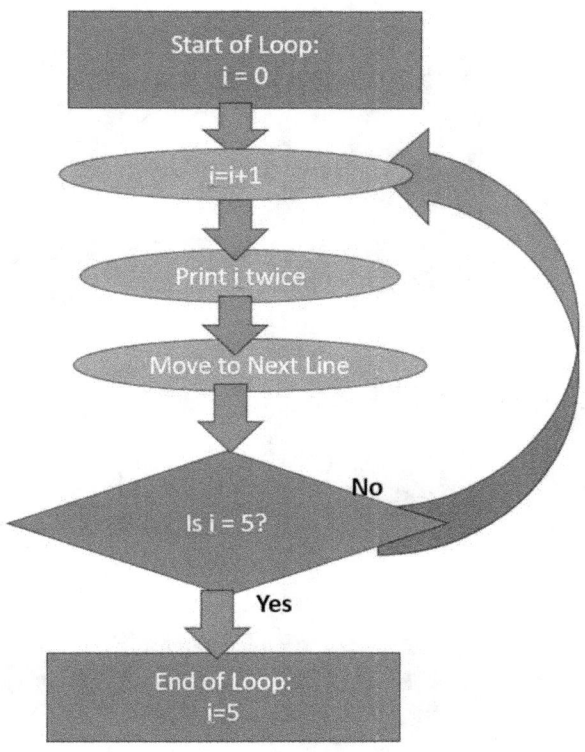

Challenge 87

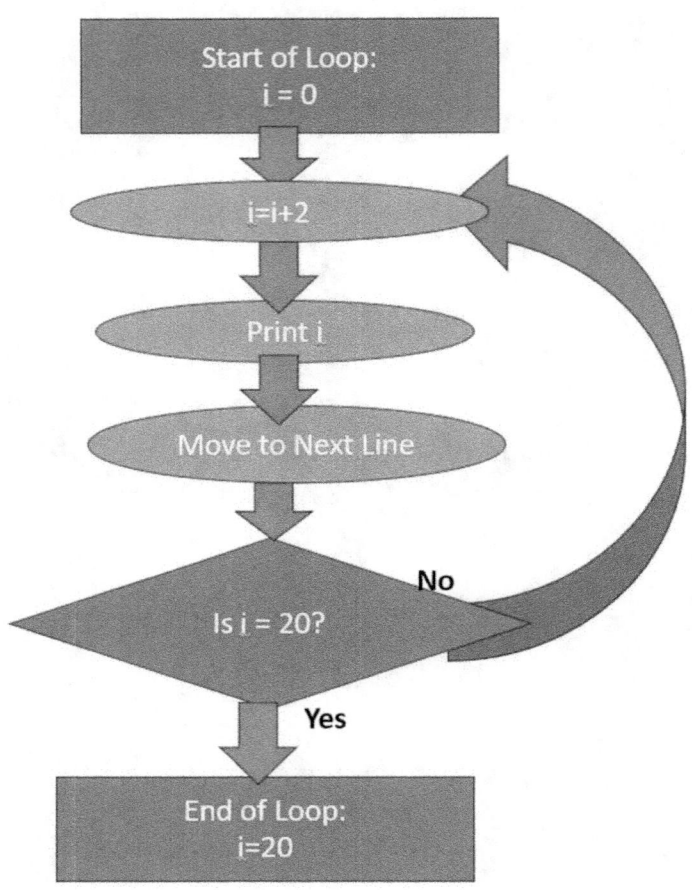

Challenge 88

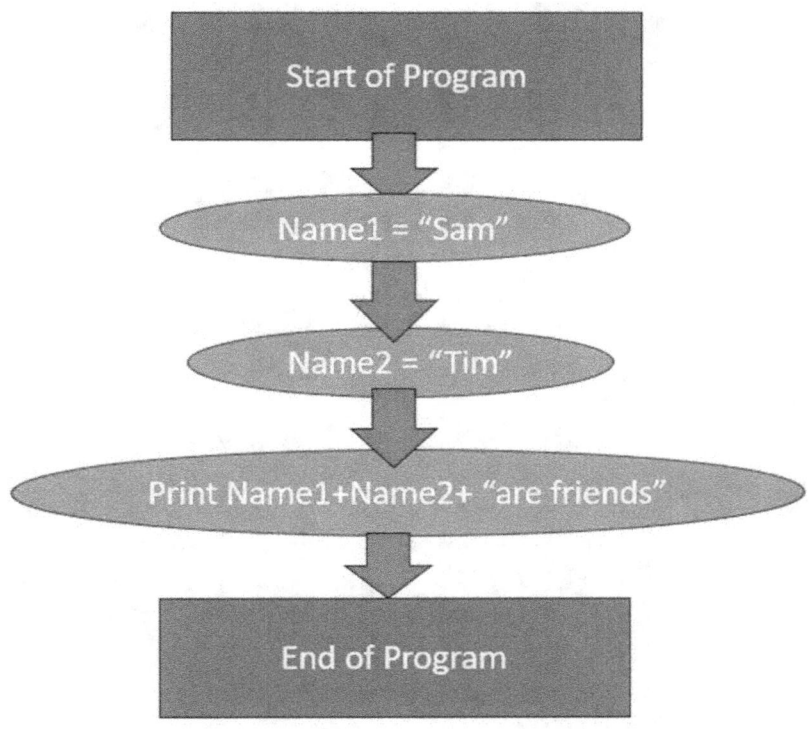

Challenge 89

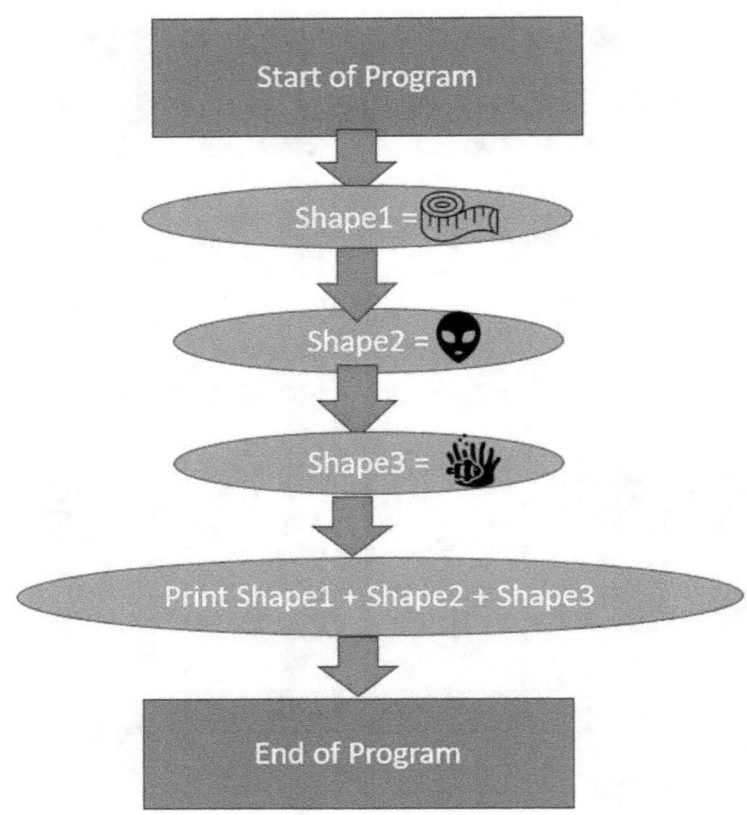

Challenge 90

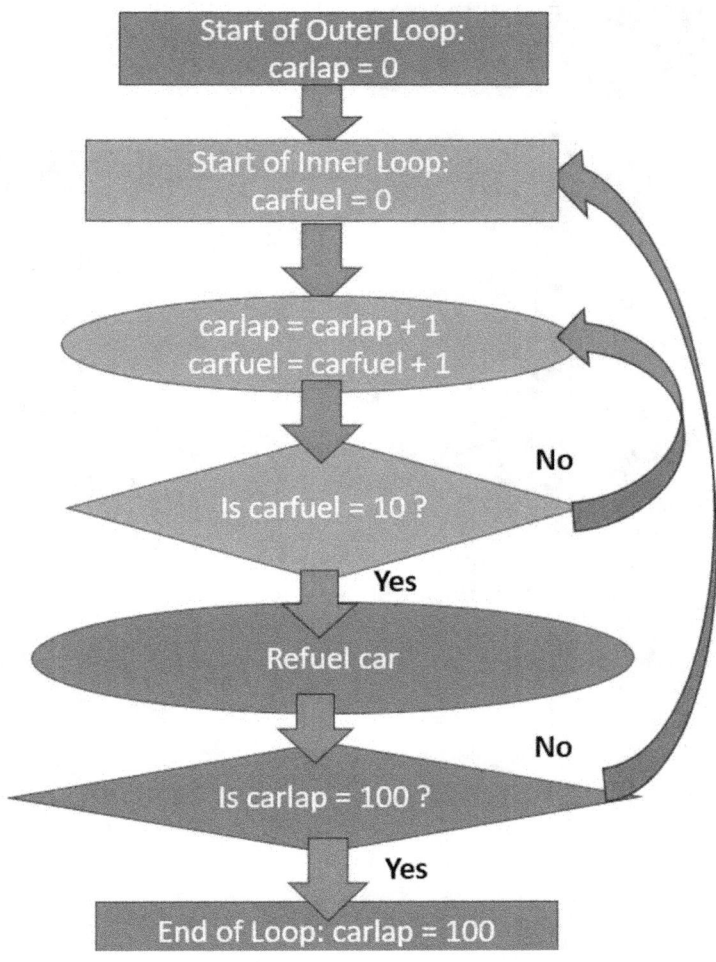

Challenge 91

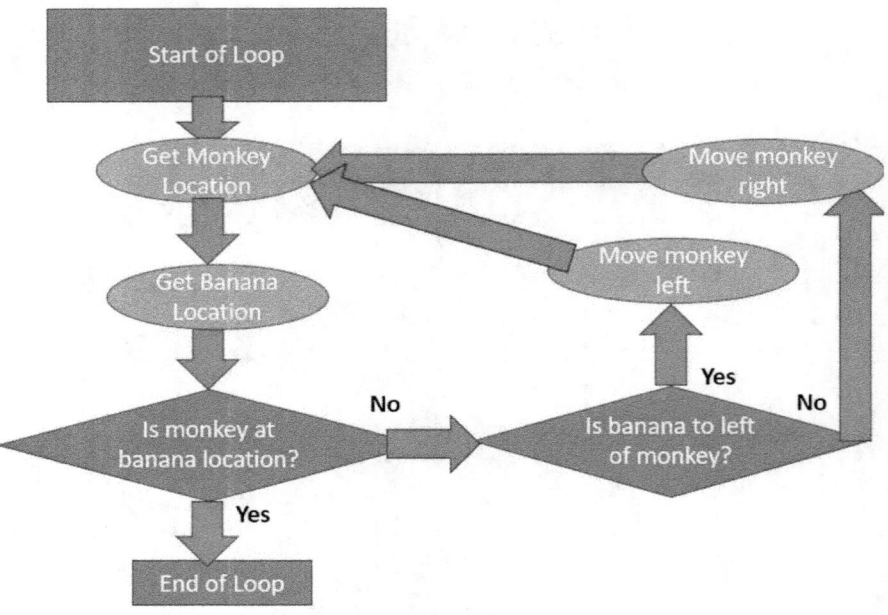

Challenge 92

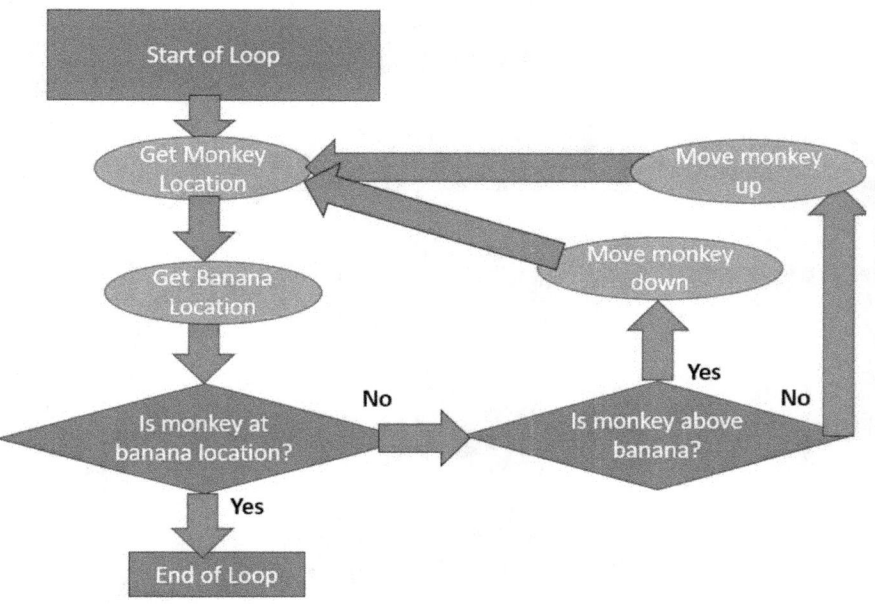

Challenge 93

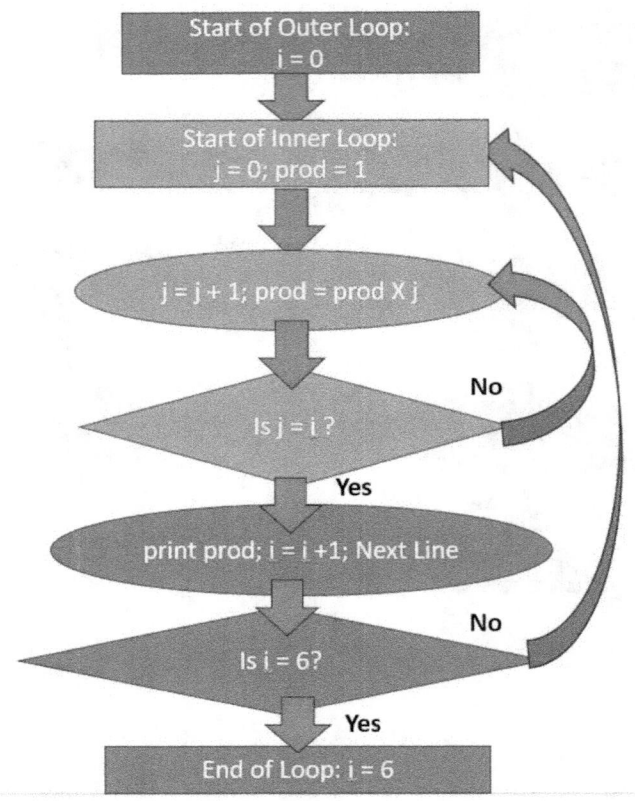

Answers

The Search for that Elusive Banana

Challenge 2

Challenge 3

Challenge 4

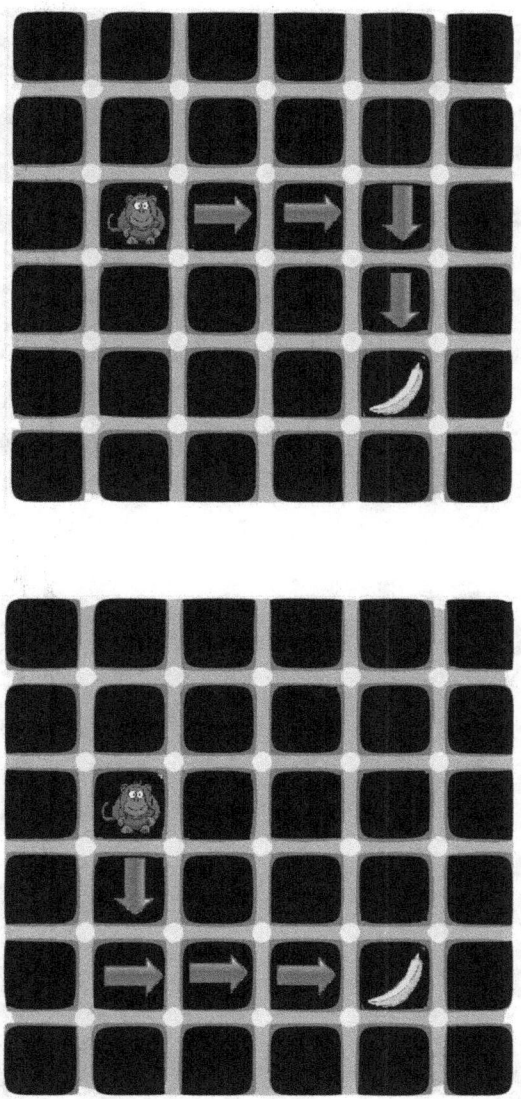

Challenge 5

Challenge 6

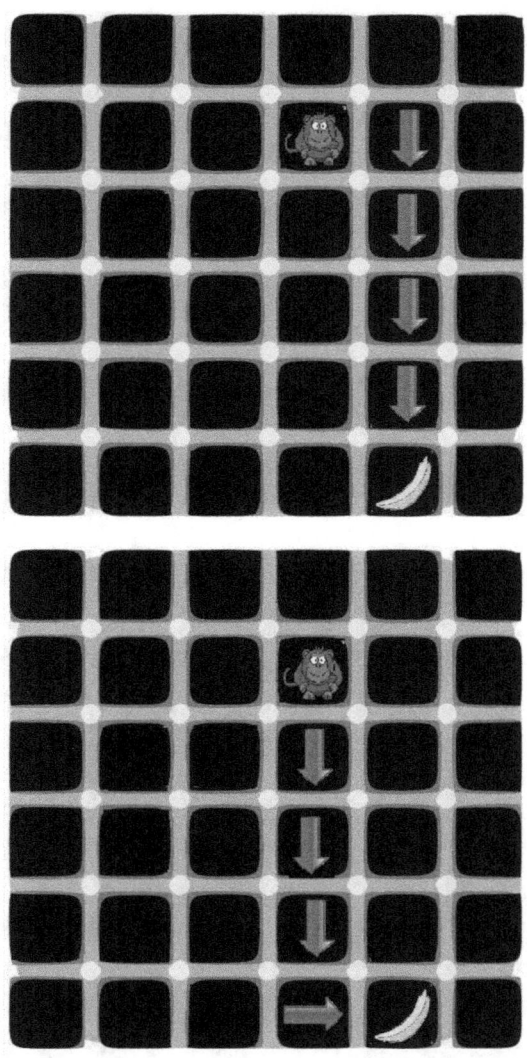

Challenge 7

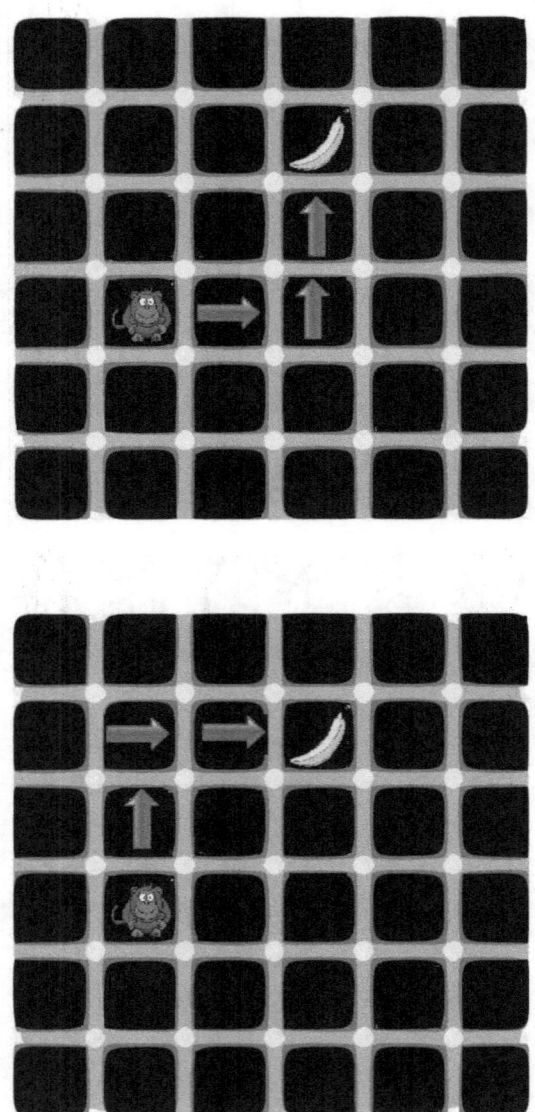

Challenge 8

Challenge 9

Challenge 10

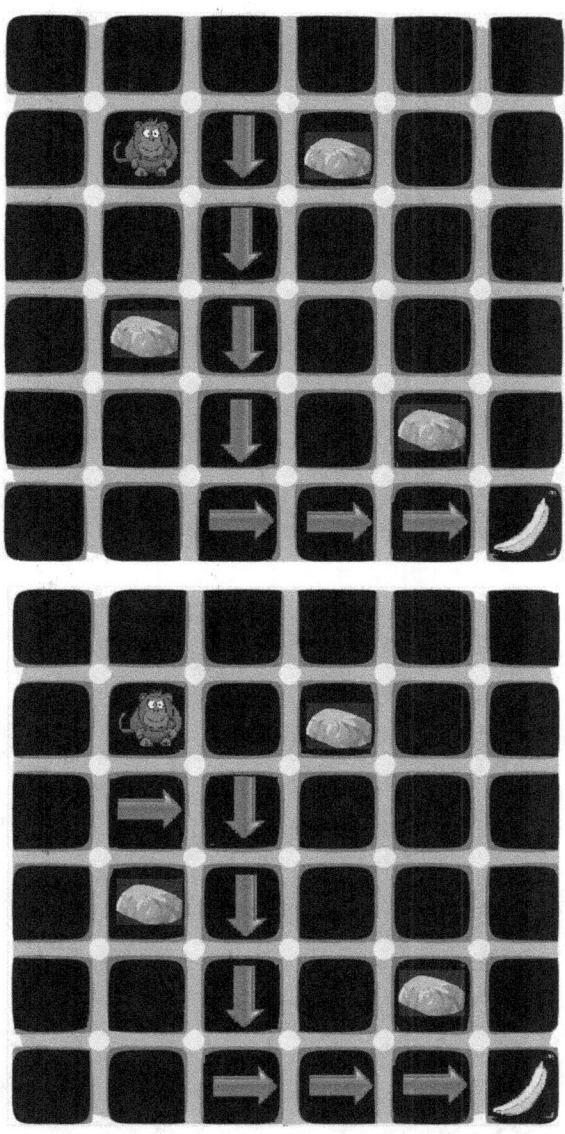

Challenge 11

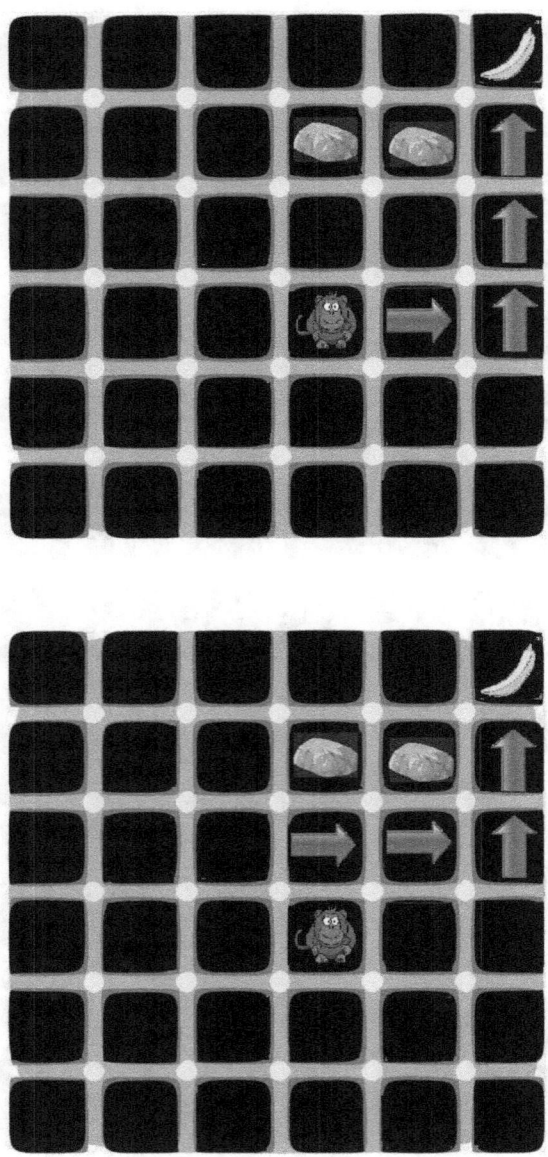

Challenge 12

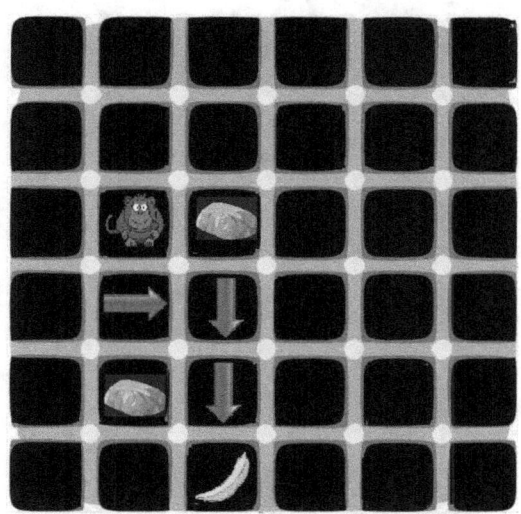

Challenge 13

Challenge 14

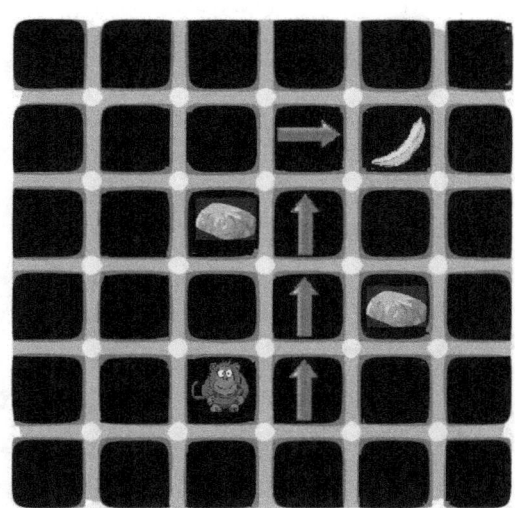

Challenge 15

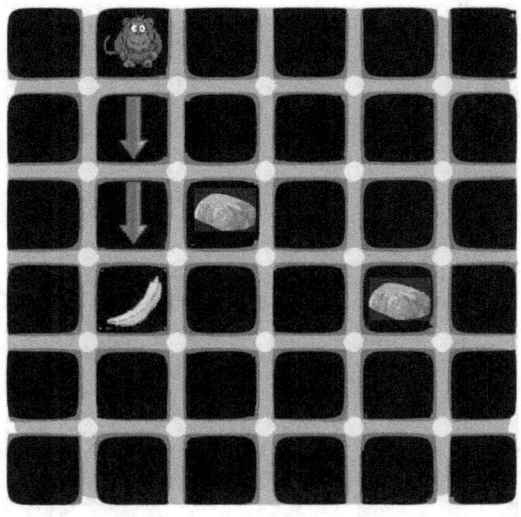

Taxi Please

Challenge 16

Challenge 17

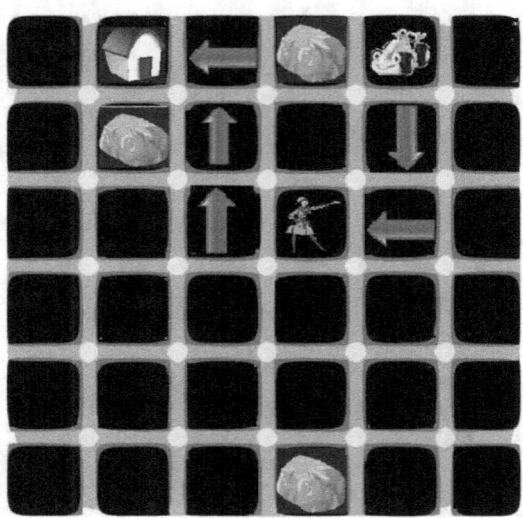

Challenge 18

Challenge 19

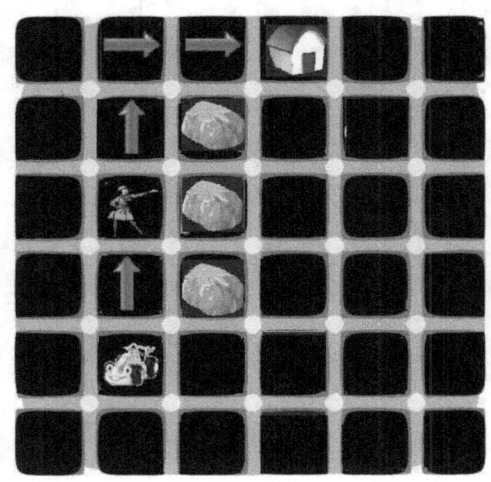

Challenge 20

Challenge 21

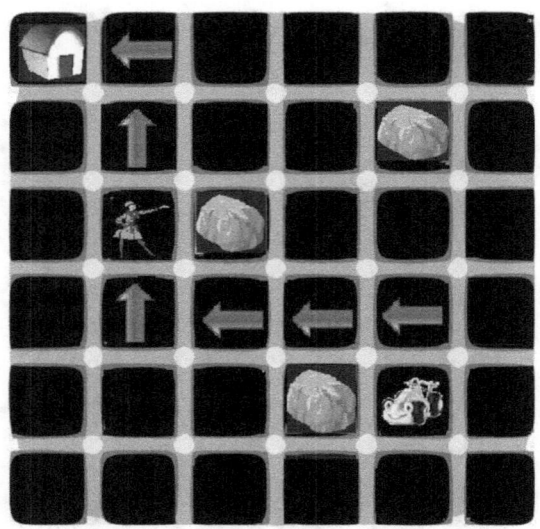

Challenge 22

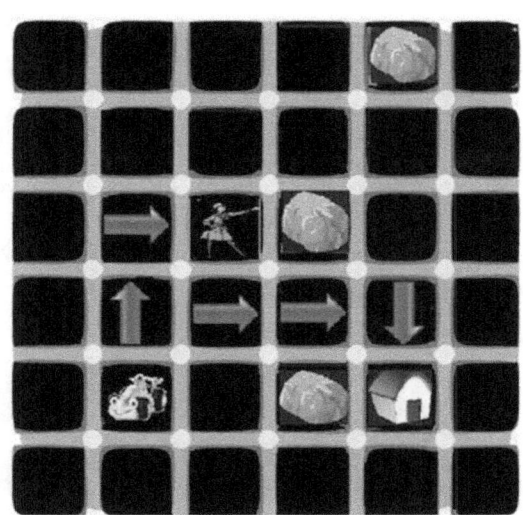

Challenge 23

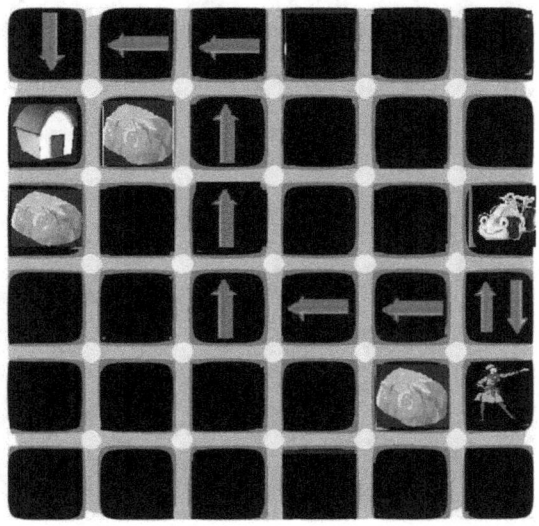

Challenge 24

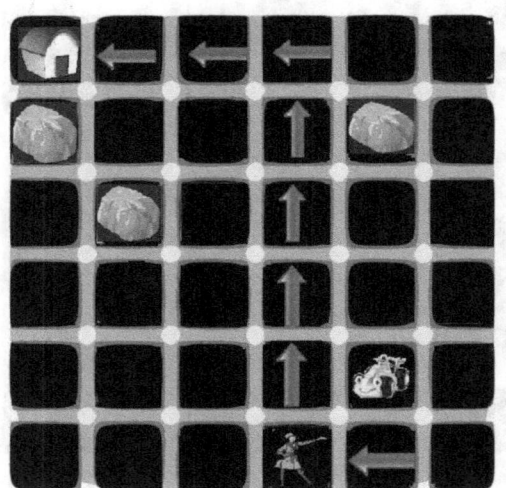

Challenge 25

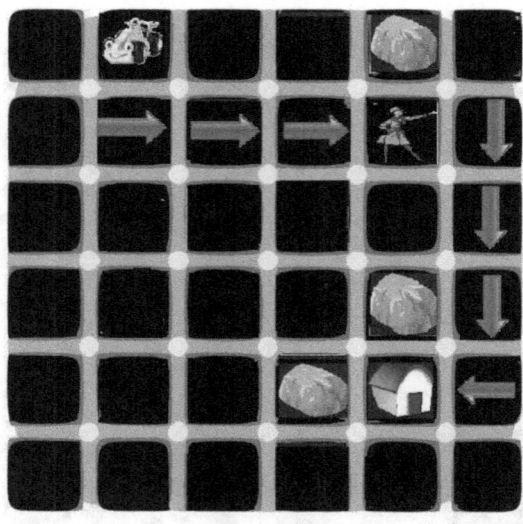

Challenge 26

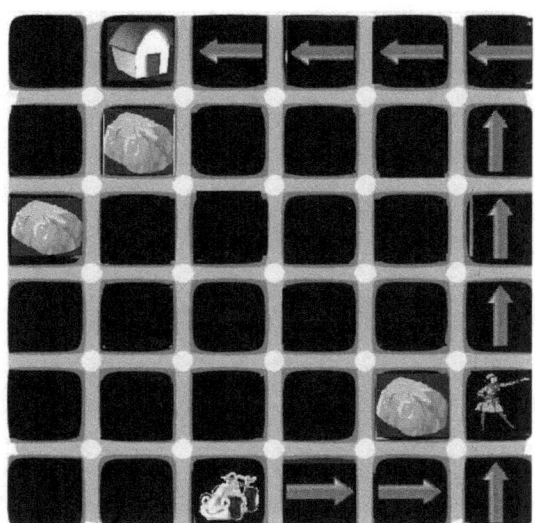

Challenge 27

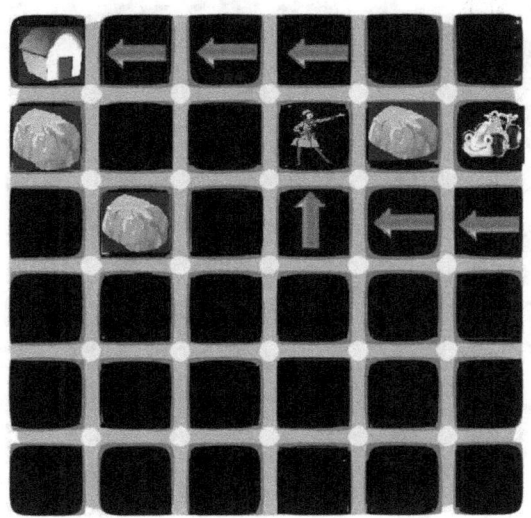

Challenge 28

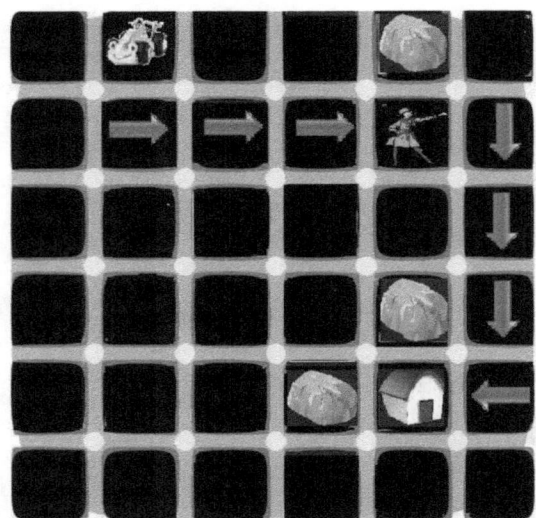

Challenge 29

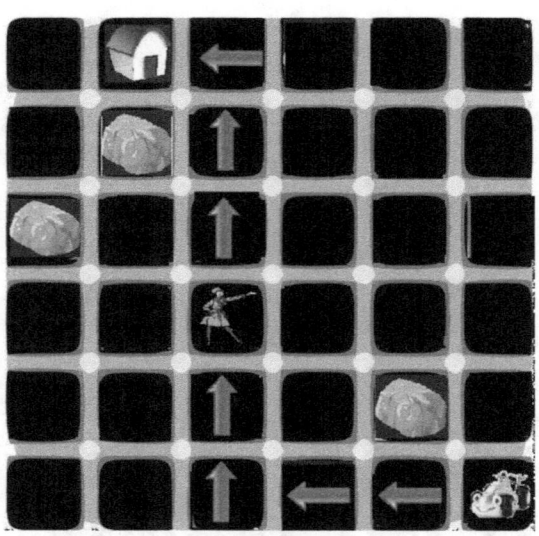

Challenge 30

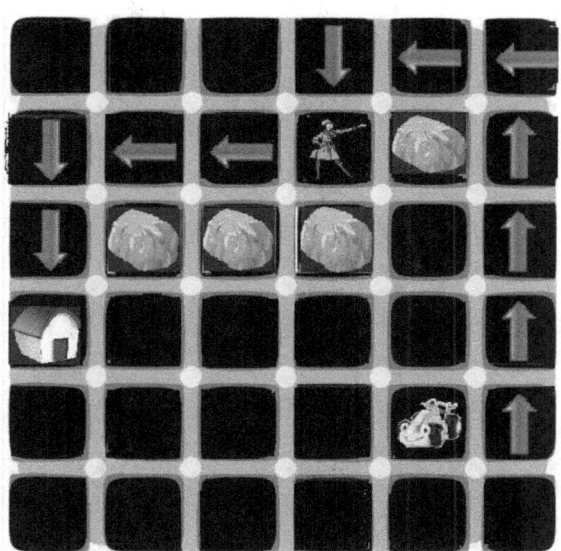

Challenge 31

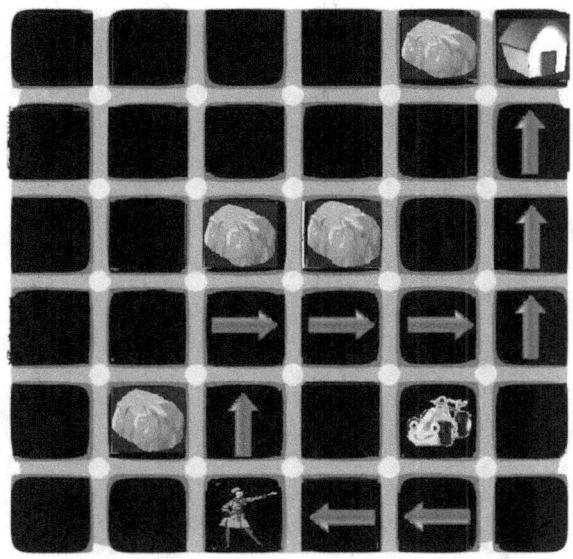

Challenge 32

Challenge 33

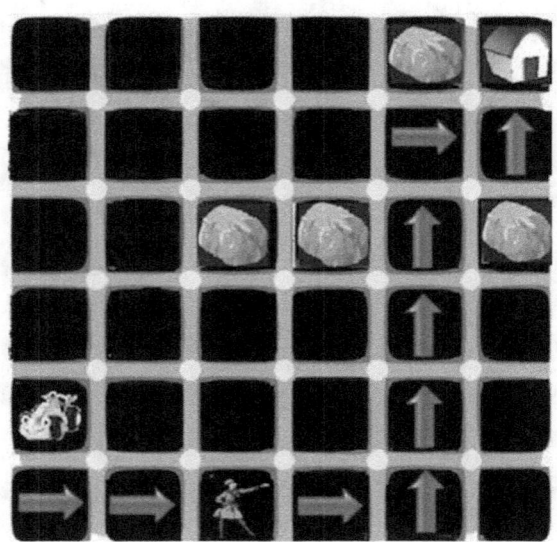

Challenge 34

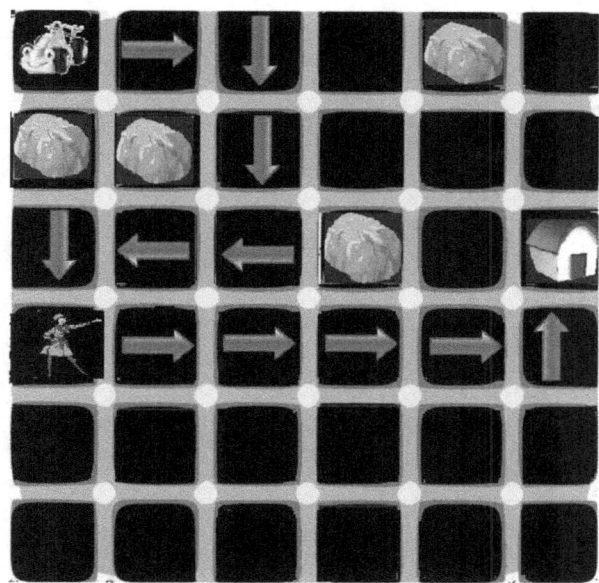

Challenge 35

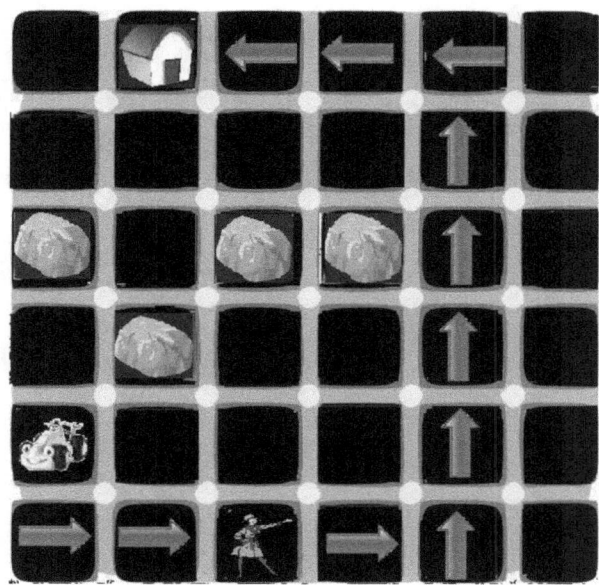

Number Key Challenge - Answers

36. 1 + 7 = 8
37. 37 X 2 = 74
38. 50 X 7 = 350
39. 87+2 = 89
40. 6 X 7 = 42
41. 999 + 89 = 1088
42. 22 X 22 = 484
43. 65 + 92 = 157
44. 1 X 33 = 33
45. 856 X 8 = 6848

Square:

46. $1^2 = 1$
47. $33^2 = 1089$
48. $30^2 = 900$
49. $17^2 = 289$
50. $11^2 = 121$
51. $13^2 = 169$
52. $51^2 = 2601$
53. $60^2 = 3600$
54. $18^2 = 324$
55. $80^2 = 6400$

Remainder:

56. 31%6 = 1
57. 185 % 5 = 0
58. 73%8 = 1
59. 73%2 = 1

60. 31%9 = 4
61. 18%5 = 3
62. 45
63. 177
64. 676
65. 22
66. 70
67. 270

68.

 (42)

69.

 (424)

70.

 (121)

71.

 (4)

72.

 (2023)

Loops

Challenge 73

The answer to the challenge is below. As we can see from the above visual, the value of the counter i is printed every time. The counter is incremented by 1 till it reaches a value of 20.

The loop stops when i reaches its end value of 20.

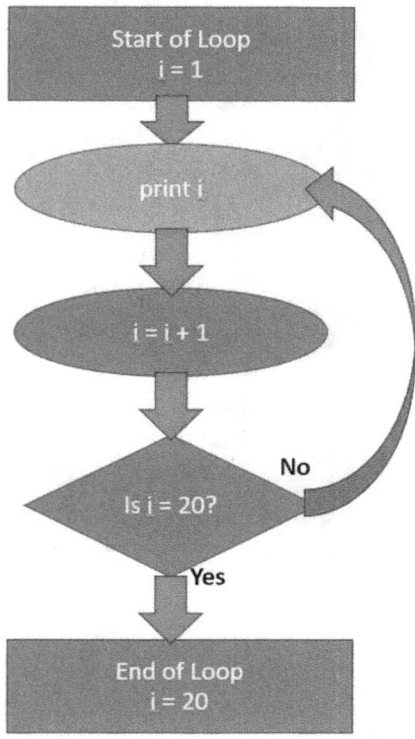

Challenge 74

The answer to the challenge is below. As we can see from the visual, the value of the counter i is printed every time. The counter is incremented by 2 till it exceeds a value of 30.

The loop stops when i is greater than 30.

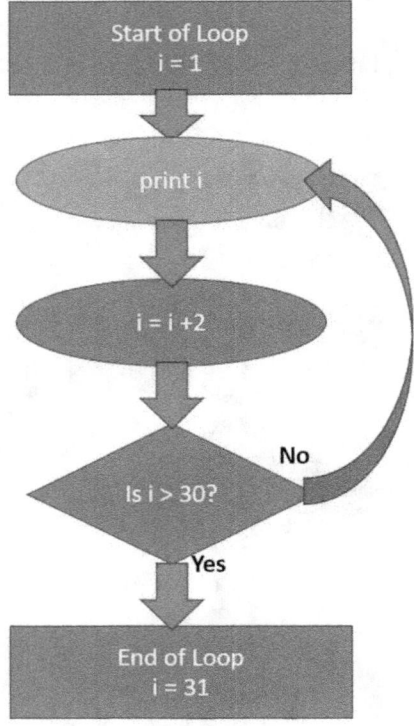

Challenge 75

The answer is below again. The visual below shows that each time we race the car around the track, we increase the counter by 1. The counter in this case is named **carloop**. Once **carloop** reaches 10, the program stops and there's no need to race the car around the track anymore.

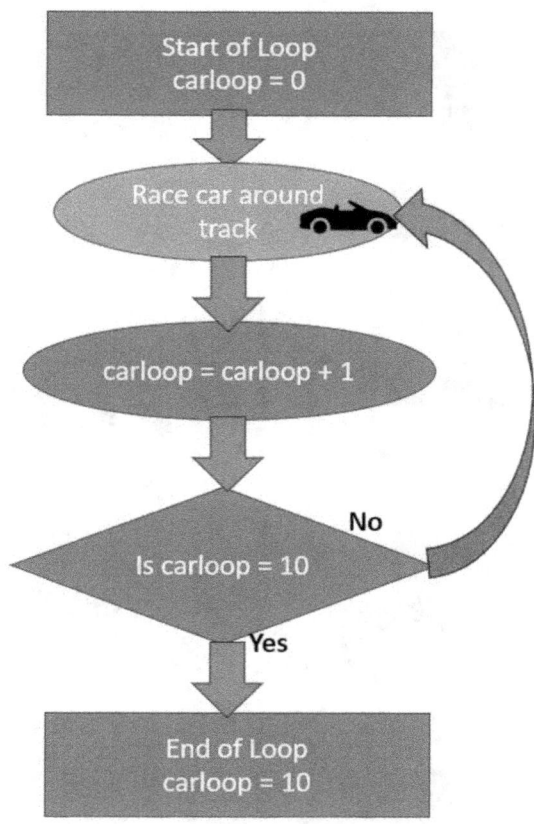

Challenge 76

The answer is below again. The visual below shows that each time the spacecraft orbits Mars, we increase the counter by 1. The counter in this case is named **marsorbit**. Once **marsorbit** reaches 5, the program stops and there's no need to race the car around the track anymore.

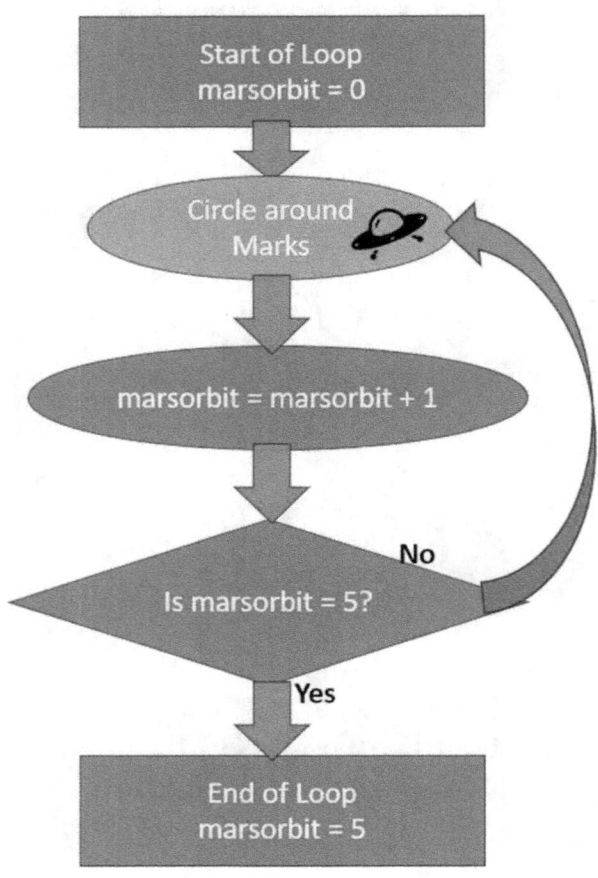

Challenge 77

The answer is below again. The visual below shows that the pattern is printed on the screen each time the counter increases. The counter in this case is named **i**. There is an additional step where the cursor moves to the next line to ensure that the pattern is only printed once each line. Once **i** reaches 100, the program stops and there's no need to race the car around the track anymore.

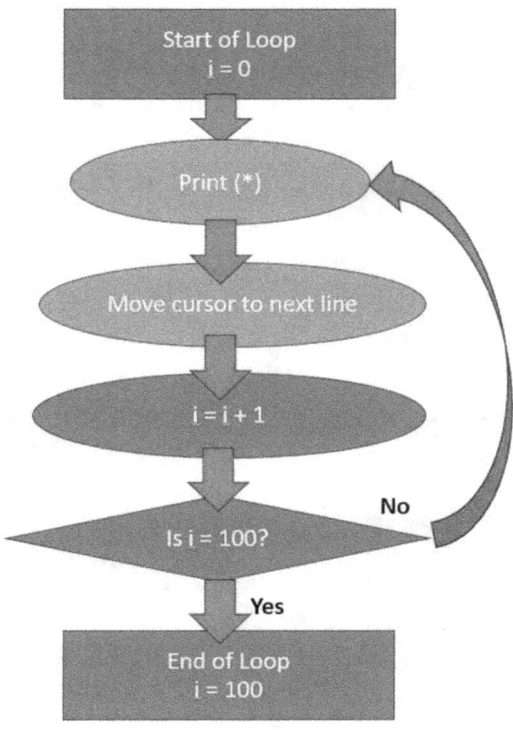

Nested Loops

Challenge 78

The answer to this question is below. The inner loop in green counts the number of bends that happen in each lap. Once the number of bends reaches three, we resume the outer loop and increase the number of laps by 1. This happens till 100 laps are complete.

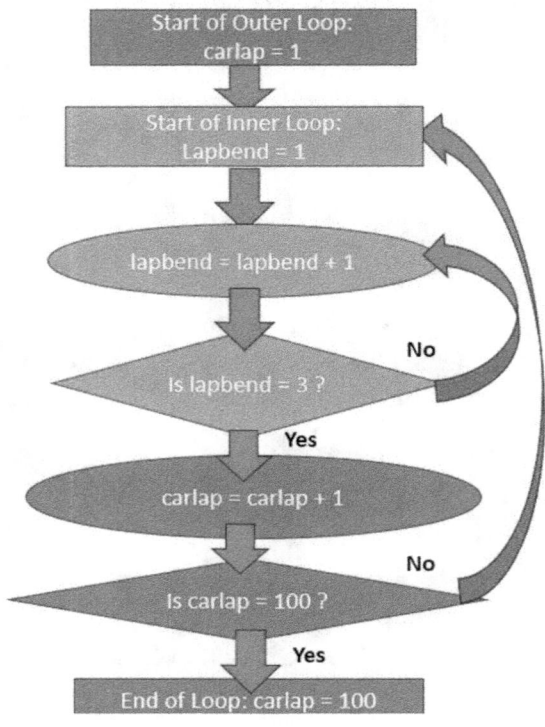

Challenge 79

Output:

1

3

6

10

15

21

28

36

45

55

Challenge 80

The completed flowchart is below. The outer loop has a counter i, which goes from 1 to 10. The counter is incremented by 1 each time and the cursor is moved to the next line.

The green inner loop has a counter j, which goes from 1 to 1. Every time it is incremented by 1, j is printed on the screen to achieve the required pattern.

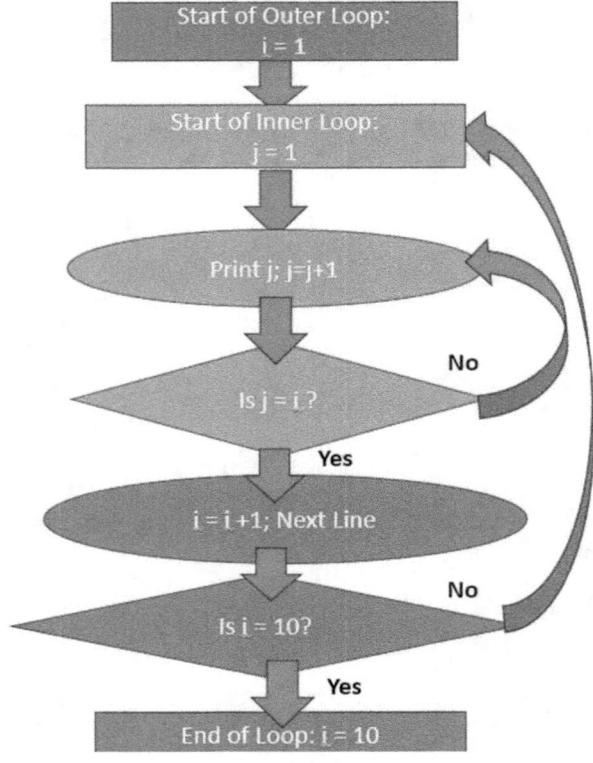

Challenge 81

The answer below is similar to the previous problem. We just print the character * on the screen in the inner loop (instead of the number j).

We do this for 6 iterations of outer loop to achieve 6 lines of output.

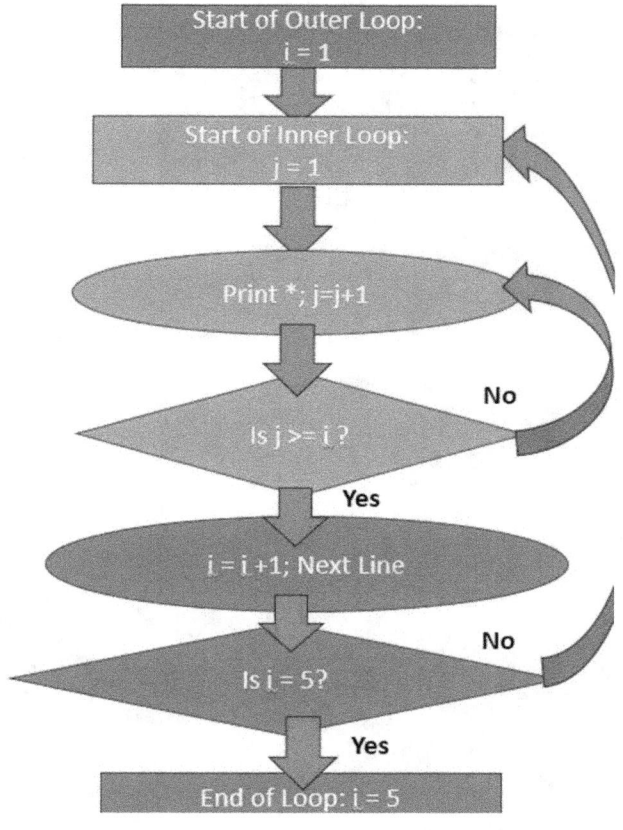

Conditional Loops

Challenge 82

Below is the completed loop. The loop starts with a heads counter of 0. The counter is increased by 1 each time the coin is tossed, and it is heads. Once the heads counter reaches 5, the loop ends. If it is not 5 yet, the loop starts again with another coin toss.

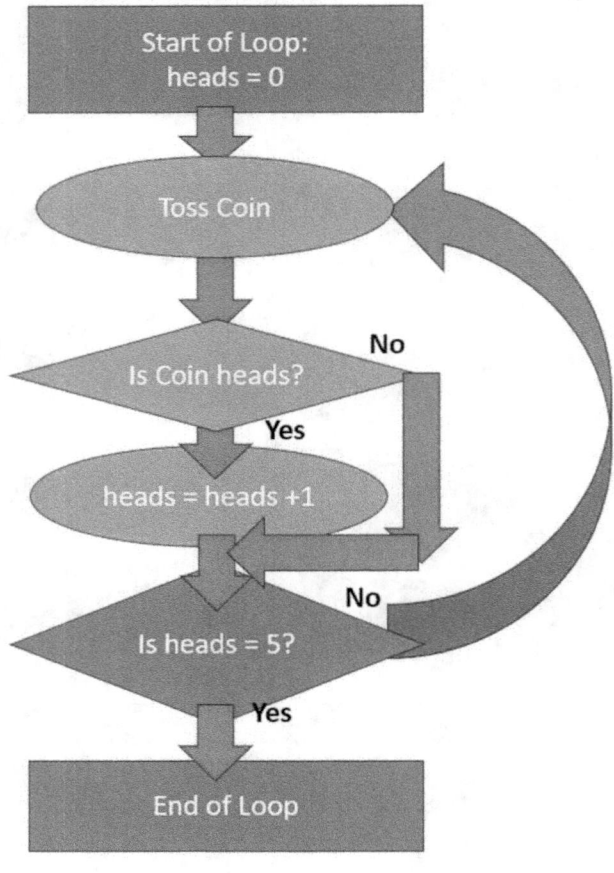

Challenge 83

Below is the completed loop.

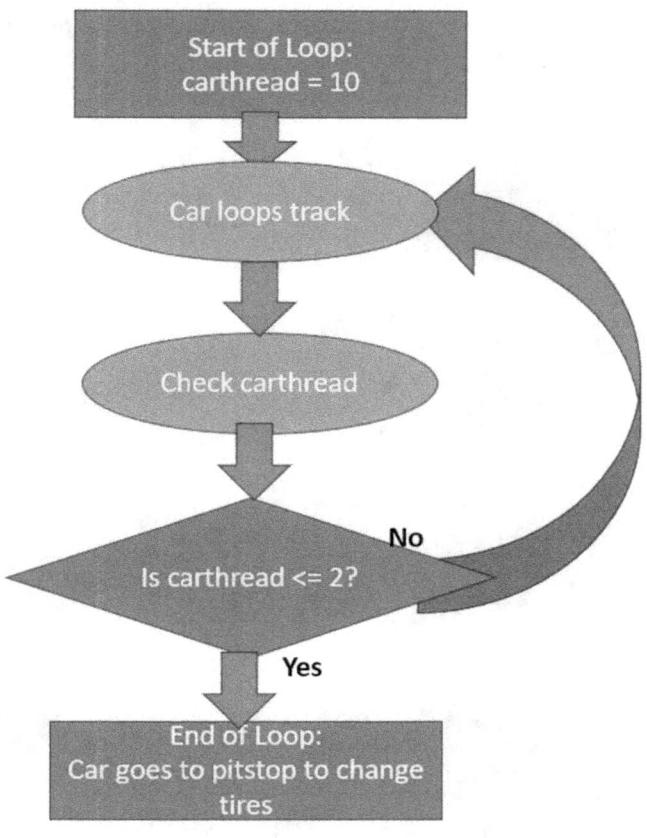

Challenge 84

Below is the completed loop that checks if the credit balance is below $100 after each transaction. If not, the customer is allowed to make additional transactions and then the **transactionamount** is subtracted from **creditbalance**.

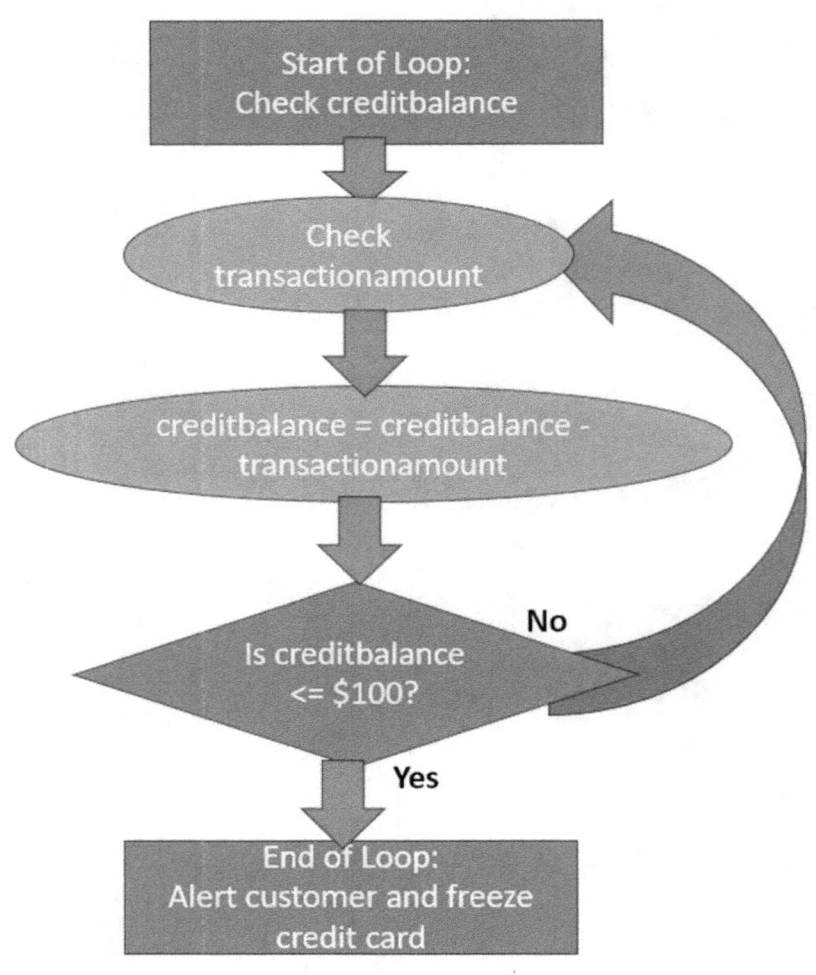

Programming Challenges

Find the outputs for the following loops:

Challenge 85

Output:

/
 /
  /
   /
    /
     /
      /
       /
        /
         /

Challenge 86

Output:

11

22

33

44

55

Challenge 87
Output:

2

4

6

8

10

12

14

16

18

20

Challenge 88

Output:

Sam and Tim are friends.

Challenge 89

Output:

Challenge 90

Output:

Car refuels every 10 laps; ends race after 100 laps.

Challenge 91

Output:

This is a 2D monkey-banana map.

Monkey goes to right if banana is to the right.

Monkey goes left if banana is to the left.

Program ends when monkey reaches banana.

Challenge 92

Output:

This is a 2D monkey-banana map.

Monkey goes up if banana is higher.

Monkey goes down if banana is lower.

Program ends when monkey reaches banana.

Challenge 93

Output:

1

2

6

24

120

720

www.ingramcontent.com/pod-product-compliance
Lightning Source LLC
Chambersburg PA
CBHW060147230426
43661CB00003B/610